# Ethics for Young People

Everett, Charles Carroll

# ETHICS

FOR

# YOUNG PEOPLE.

BY

## C. C. EVERETT

Bussey Professor of Theology in Harvard University; Author of "The Science of Thought," "Poetry, Comedy and Duty," etc.

———————•✦•———————

BOSTON
GINN AND COMPANY
1893

# TABLE OF CONTENTS

---

---

# ETHICS FOR YOUNG PEOPLE.

## CHAPTER I.

### THE RELATION OF ETHICS TO OTHER STUDIES.

ETHICS is the science of morality. By science is here meant the systematic treatment of any object of study.

Ethics is called a science, because it presents the principles of morality in a systematic form, and seeks to find the basis upon which they rest.

A comparison with other departments of study may make more clear the nature of the subjects of which Ethics treats.

There are three kinds of science.

There are in the first place *the sciences that treat of facts*, of their relations to one another, and of the laws that govern them. It is to these that the name science is more commonly given.

These sciences have to do with facts past and future as well as present.

Geology pictures to us the state of the earth long ages ago, and astronomy, that of the heavens. The astronomer can also foretell the position of the planets at any moment in the future, if he cares to make the calculation; and the geologist can foretell the future of the world, though with less exactness as to time.

*To these sciences one thing is as important as another* if it illustrates the working of a general law. The insect, the dust that fills the air, in a word, anything may be an object of study.

You would hardly believe, for instance, how much the frog has contributed to the knowledge of the world.

The web of the frog's foot is so thin and transparent that under the microscope the blood can be seen moving. Looked at in this way the blood is perceived to be not a mere fluid. You can see what look like circular discs borne along something like the cakes of ice that are carried by a stream in a freshet. In this way the student of anatomy can learn in a moment more about the circulation of the blood than can be taught in any other way in a much longer time. Moreover, what he sees he *knows* as he does not know what is merely told him, just as, though you may have learned in books about the hippopotamus, for instance, the sight of one first gives you real knowledge about it.

Further, Professor Frog is not merely a teacher, he is a discoverer. The changes seen in the blood when the web of the foot is inflamed, taught more in regard to the nature of inflammation than had ever been known before.

Through the frog, galvanism was discovered. Galvani, an Italian, noticed that the leg of a dead frog that was being prepared for the table twitched violently under certain circumstances. This observation led to examination and experiment, and, as I just said, galvanism was discovered.

In addition to all this, so much has been learned from the frog in relation to the nervous system, that it would take almost a book by itself to describe it.

Let any boy think of all this when he is tempted to throw a stone at a frog, and ask himself whether he is likely ever to do so much good as frogs have done.

You probably know how Franklin discovered that the lightning is a form of electricity by flying a kite in a thunderstorm. I remind you of these things to show that there is nothing so trivial that it may' not have an interest for science.

It would be a good plan for all boys and girls to study some science, so that they could understand and take an interest in flowers or rocks, or some other natural objects. Then, wherever they went, they would find something to occupy their minds. They would learn to keep their eyes open, so that they would see in the world a thousand things that they would never have dreamed of otherwise.

I repeat that what is commonly called " science " treats of facts, and that all sorts of facts are important to it.

## CHAPTER II.

### THE RELATION OF ETHICS TO OTHER STUDIES.

#### *Continued.*

THERE are, in the second place, other sciences that treat *of the means by which certain desirable ends may be reached.*

Health is one of the most desirable things in the world, and thus there is a science called Hygiene which treats of the methods by which health may be preserved.

The health of the state is perhaps more important than that of the citizen; so there is the science of Political Economy which shows the conditions on which the prosperity of the state depends.

Indeed, there is nothing that we try to do which has not or might not have its science. There is a science of music, and a science of painting. There is also a science even of base-ball. The kind of curve that the pitcher must give the ball so that it will change its course just in time to baffle the stroke of the batter would be a matter of very interesting scientific research.

Such a study is called an art when the application of principles is more dwelt upon than the principles themselves. Thus we have both the science and the art of speaking, of painting, and of other matters which men try to accomplish.

If a man would really accomplish anything he must

generally add to the science or the art what can best be called a "knack." By this I mean the skill that comes mostly by practice, added to a certain mental fitness or common-sense. A student of medicine may know all about diseases and cures, who could hardly tell the measles from the small-pox when he first saw it. The boy is taught how to pitch a ball; but at first trying it goes all awry. All at once it goes just as it should, while he seems to himself to be doing just what he did before.

The sciences that teach us the conditions upon which depend the ends that we wish to bring about, we may take together and call the science of means.

A third kind of science *shows the ends which are in themselves desirable.* This is the science that is called Ethics.

A man, for instance, wishes to succeed in business. His studies and his practical training have fitted him to do this. He seeks out all the methods by which he may reach success. He shrinks from no labor of mind, or, if need be, of body, for this end. In all this he is right. We admire skill, industry and pluck. There is, however, one kind of means that he may not use. He may not stoop to fraud of any kind. He *may* desire and seek wealth; he *must* desire and seek honor and honesty. These are among the ends that morality insists upon, and that may not be sacrificed to anything else.

Thus, while the first class of sciences that I named has to do with all facts, and the second only with

those that help or hinder the reaching of certain ends,
Ethics has to do *with the ends themselves*.

Ethics is thus the science of living; not of living
healthily and long, — the science of Hygiene has to do
with that, — but of living well; that is, in such a way as
to make life really worth living.

# CHAPTER III.

## THE RELATION OF THE DIFFERENT SCIENCES TO REALITY.

THE science of facts *has changed greatly men's thought of the world.* Men used to think that the earth stands still and that the sun revolves about it. They knew nothing of steam as a means of power, and were ignorant of many things which are so familiar to us, that a schoolboy knows more about them to-day than the wisest men who lived long ago.

This kind of science *has not changed the world*, it has simply found out about the world. The facts and laws of which it treats were the same then as now, whether men knew them or not.

Men were, for example, whirling around the sun with the earth, when they thought that the sun and the stars were whirling about them. Electricity was as active then as now, though it had not been set to work. The laws of the universe have not changed; only men's notions about them have changed.

There are doubtless a great many laws of the world which we do not yet know; and a great many elements and forces which we have not yet discovered; so that the people of future ages will know as much more than we do as we know more than our forefathers.

By science, then, we are slowly learning to see the world as it is. The change is not in it but in us.

The science of means and the arts that spring from it *have really changed the world.* This power to change the world constitutes a great difference between the science of means and that of facts. Think of all the cities and railways that have been built, of all the forests that have been cut down, of all the instruments that have been invented, because men have been bringing about the ends that seemed desirable by what seemed to them the best means.

Men have not always used the best means; they have merely used the best that they knew.

The best ways were always the best ways, even before men found them out, or before they were able to use them. The savage used to kindle his fires by rubbing two dry sticks together till they became so hot that they burst into a blaze. This was the best way for him because it was the best way that he knew. It was, however, not really the best way, for a friction match would have been better, if he had had knowledge and wit to invent it. The laws of Hygiene have been always the same, though cities have invited disease by being undrained and filthy. The principles of Political Economy, though there have been foolish and harmful laws and social customs, are always the same.

*The best ways are thus always the same,* just as the laws and forces of the world are the same. The science of means is simply finding out these best ways; just as the science of facts is finding out the truth about the world.

The science of ends has also *changed the world very*

*much.* In some former times men were much more cruel than they are now, and cared less for others, except when these others were their friends. Those who were strong often robbed or murdered the weak or held them in slavery. They cared very little how others lived. Now there is more helpfulness, as well as less cruelty, in the world. Many are interested that the sick should have better homes. There is still a great deal of selfishness and cruelty in the world, but this care for others has removed many of the evils of life. We are as comfortable and happy as we are to-day, because among those who have lived before us there were many who did not seek merely their own good.

*The laws of right doing, also, are always the same,* whether men know and obey them or not.

One difference between the science of ends and other kinds of science is, that men have not only to learn what is right, but have also to be willing to do it. If men really want to accomplish anything, and really know the best way of doing it, they will hardly fail to take this way. On the contrary, they may know what is right and yet be unwilling to do it.

If one does not know what is right, he cannot be expected to do it, or blamed if he does not do it. Though the life of love and of helpfulness, of care for the stranger and for the weak, is and always has been the true life, it was not the fault of the savage, living in barbarism, that he did not follow it, if he knew nothing better than his own cruel way of living.

The science of morality, like the science of facts, *seeks*

*to learn what is.* It does not invent the laws of right, it finds them. The laws of right do not grow. They have always existed, as truly as the laws which govern the motion of the planets.

Future ages will probably look down upon our barbarism, as we do upon that of the savage. It will not be because the laws of right have become different. It will be simply because men will have learned more of what is right, and will have become more willing to practice what they know.

## CHAPTER IV.

### ETHICS AS A WAY OF LIFE.

THE word Ethics is derived from a Greek word [1] that means custom or habit. The word Morality is derived from a Latin word [2] having a like meaning. Thus both words meant at first what is habitual. Habit and custom, here, probably refer, not to the custom of a people, but, that of men and women taken separately.

*Everybody has a way of life* which has become to a certain extent habitual with him.

In regard to a person that you know very well, you form some idea of his way of life, as really as you do of his personal appearance. You know pretty well what to expect of him. You know that you can trust one person and that you cannot trust another; that one boy will probably be rude, and another courteous; that one will probably have his lesson, and that another will not; that one will join in some piece of unkind mischief, and that another will not.

You sometimes hear a story which you do not believe about some one whom you know very well You say, "It is not like him, he would never do so in the world." Sometimes we judge the representations in novels in this way. We say of the act of some charac-

---

[1] 'Ηθος

[2] *Mos*, in the plural *Mores.*

ter, " It is not natural." We have learned to know the character so well that we feel that the author has made a mistake.

This "way of life" shows itself in the occupations and amusements which different persons prefer. Some young people would rather play than read; others would rather read than play. Some enter heartily into their work or their play. Some are lazy and indifferent in both. Some join heartily in one, but not in the other.

The difference in people's ways reaches to matters much more minute than those that I have named. You cannot describe a man's 'way' any more than you can his face, but you know it all the same; and his looks and his ways together make up your general notion of him.

It is this difference in people's ways that is largely the reason why you like to be with one person rather than with another. Friends are apt to be those whose ways are similar or at least harmonious.

People sometimes change their ways so that they become better or more agreeable. Thus a person is sometimes said to " mend his ways."

It is a poor excuse for one's negligence or selfishness to say, "Oh, it is his way." This makes the matter worse rather than better.

Though the word Ethics referred originally simply to the habits and ways of different people, it soon came to mean a study of the best way of living; that is, of the ends and methods of life that are most to be desired.

## CHAPTER V.

### THE ETHICS OF CUSTOM.

At all times the manner of life of the individual has been greatly influenced by the customs of the society in which he lived. Our lives to-day are shaped to a great extent by the lives of those about us.

In the earlier times, *this law of custom was the only standard of morality.* What was customary was recognized as right, and was often believed to rest on divine authority. A large part of life was thus determined by custom. In what was not thus determined a man could do what he pleased.

Many things that are really very wrong were thus justified by custom, and were sometimes even commanded by it. Such have been, sometimes, the putting the aged to death, which was required by custom among the Fiji Islanders; and the murder or the neglect of children, which was permitted. A Roman father could bring up his child or not, as it pleased him. He had the power of life or death over his family. Slavery has been thus justified, and has often been very cruel. You know how perilous it is, even to-day, for a stranger to find himself in the midst of barbarians, as in the heart of Africa. The barbarians feel it neither a wrong to slay strangers nor a duty to protect them. They do in this matter just what they happen to feel like doing.

The morality of custom is thus *a very imperfect kind of morality*, both in what it commands and in what it allows.

The morality of custom has, however, been of great service to the world. The customs of civilized men have, in some respects, improved from age to age, and these better customs have tended to make men better, and thus to introduce still better customs.

Suppose we all had to start for ourselves, without finding any principles of action recognized in the world, we should be much worse than we actually are. If we each had to learn for himself, that it is wrong to kill and to steal, for instance, many more would fail to learn the lesson than do now.

Many persons at the present day recognize no moral standard except that of the custom in the community in which they live. They are in this like those who lived in more barbarous times; only the custom which they obey is often, though not always, very much better than that of the barbarians.

The social customs of the present day represent the result of the lives of all who have lived before us. Their way of living makes the customs of the community in which we live.

These customs are different among different sets of persons, even in the same town. It is the average morality that determines the lives of most.

This average of custom in morals is like the mode, or fashion, in dress. A lady asks, for instance, "What are they wearing this season?"

The lowest and worst form of the morality of custom takes shape in the proverb which tells us that " When we are in Rome we must do as the Romans do." — This proverb commonly means that a man need never try to be better than those about him.

If men had always acted according to this rule, the world would never have improved; for the world improves by the help of some, in every age, who are better than those about them, and thus raise the general level of life. If men had always acted in the spirit of this proverb, there would have been no heroes, for the hero is one who is heroic: that is, who is braver and nobler than other men.

You would not think much of a boy or girl who is always ready to do what the rest do, whether it is good or bad, wise or foolish. Yet there are a good many people, old and young, who act upon this principle.

On the other hand, the morality of custom keeps many men from sinking to lives much lower than they actually live. If it does nothing to make the world better, it often prevents it from growing worse. It helps to keep society from losing the ground that it has already gained.

It is a good rule of life that *one should never fall below the average morality* of the society in which one lives.

This is a pretty low standard, but we shall have higher ones as we go on. If all would act according to this rule, however, we should escape drunkenness, vice, dishonesty, impurity, and many other bad things which are the sediment and mud of social life.

## CHAPTER VI.

### THE IMPERFECTION OF THE ETHICS OF CUSTOM.

WHILE the morality that rests on custom is better than nothing, it *is yet very imperfect.*

It represents, as we have seen, only the *average morality* of any time or place. Thus the influence of the best men is not felt in it except indirectly; that is, so far as they may in time affect the general custom. The man whose morality rests on that which prevails about him does not ask what the best men do, but what average men do; or, as it is often expressed, what " they do."

*The morality that rests upon custom is uncertain.* Customs vary in different communities, and, as we have seen, in different circles of the same community. While certain gross faults and crimes are forbidden by the average morality, the judgment in regard to other matters varies so much that one who is looking to custom to know what he should do, might easily become confused.

Further, he might live so wholly in some one circle that he should take its judgment for that of the community. Before the French Revolution, for instance, the nobles thought that their standard of right and wrong was that of the nation. They oppressed the people in many cruel ways; but when the Revolution broke out they had no support against the popular fury. Politicians have sometimes a low standard of political action which they think is the popular one, when perhaps it is one for which the best people have a contempt. In certain trades or professions there may be ways of business which contradict the general principles of honesty even as these are recognized by the world at large. In a school or college there may be a standard of public sentiment very different from that of the outside world; or in a group of scholars there may be ways of acting and of feeling which contradict the best sentiment of the school at large. One's moral sense may thus become confused and blinded.

*A morality based upon custom is variable.* As one passes from one circle to another, or from one community to another, his own morality is likely to vary with his surroundings. Many, who in a well-ordered society had lived respectable lives, have sadly fallen when they went to newer communities, where they found ways of living of a low order. When boys and girls go from their homes to school or to college, they often find a standard of thinking and of acting very different from that to which they had been used. What they had supposed wrong they sometimes find regarded as right, or at least very slightly condemned. It is often the same when they go from school out into the world.

The morality that rests upon custom *does not really belong to the man that practises it.* If he be good among the good and bad among the bad; more or less honest, according to the habits that are about him; high-minded or low-minded, according as others' minds are high or low, he has no real virtue of his own. If he have what seem to be virtues, it is by a happy accident.

A person that always does what those about him do, is like a vessel with a broken rudder, that drifts with the winds and the currents, and has no course of its own any more than the drifting sea-weed. Such a life is unworthy of any one. Every one should have some moral aim, and take the helm of his own life, and steer instead of drifting.

All of this shows the need of some principles of morality that are not dependent upon any chance companionship, and that may belong to the man himself and not merely to his surroundings.

# CHAPTER VII

## PRINCIPLES OF MORALITY.

A PRINCIPLE is a starting-point in thought or life.

Every science has principles which are its starting-points. In geometry, these first principles are called axioms. If one wishes to show that a proposition in geometry is true, he tries to trace it back to one or more axioms which nobody disputes.

It is as when a person is lost in a forest and does not know which way to go, if he can find his way back and consider afresh the general direction that he should take, he can start again with better hope of success.

Principles in morals furnish such starting-points in the activities of our life.

One may ask in regard to any proposed act or speech, "Is it right?" "Is it kind?" "Is it fair?" "Is it true?"

If these words represent the principles upon which one acts and speaks, the answer to these questions will show him what he should do.

In morals, one may have bad principles as well as good principles.

A man whose principle it is always to look out only for his own gain, whether the course he takes be right or wrong, is a man of bad principles. He asks in regard to any course, "Is it profitable?" and acts accordingly.

If one says to him, "This is not right," "This is not kind," or "This is not honest," it does not affect him. For the right, the kind, and the honest do not represent the principles upon which he acts.

A man is sometimes spoken of as unprincipled This generally means that he has bad principles.

A man may seem not to have any principles because his actions are so variable. At one moment he may speak harshly, at another pleasantly, even when the circumstances are very similar. At one time he may be generous, at another selfish; or at one time honest, at another dishonest. Thus he may seem to have no principles. It may be his principle, however, to do at any moment just what he feels like doing. This is obviously a form of selfishness, and may be a principle like any other. The weathercock is often regarded as the very ideal of fickleness. It changes its position so often that it seems the type of the lack of steadfastness. But the weathercock is not fickle. It is always true to the wind, and is thus steadfast in its relation to it. So the person of variable moods may be always true to the principle of doing what pleases him at the moment.

Persons often do not know what the principles on which they act really are. The selfish person would hardly admit, even to himself, that his principle is always to look out for himself without regard to other people. Very few persons will admit that their principle is to do always as other people do.

It would often be helpful to a man if he knew what

the principles are on which he acts. If they are poor and base he might be ashamed of them and give them up.

Other people often know what a man's principles are better than the man himself does. They know them just as we know the nature of a plant from its leaves, flowers or fruit. A man acts from his real principles, and thus he also is known by his fruit.

A boy or girl that is stingy cannot have generous principles. One whose word cannot be trusted cannot really mean to tell the truth. One who grumbles when any service is asked of him and goes to it unwillingly, cannot make it his principle to be helpful.

All this is plain enough when other people are concerned. One would think that we might apply the same method to ourselves, and find out what our own principles are by observing our actions. It would often be very helpful.

Persons who do not have distinctly good principles are apt to act, more or less, from bad principles.

It is so much easier to act selfishly than to look out for others, so much easier to go with the crowd than against the crowd, that one who does not really mean to take the better course is very apt to take the worse, without thinking anything about it.

" I did not mean to," the boy said, as we all so often say, when he had done a piece of mischief by accident. " But did you mean not to?" asked the teacher. We all do more wrong things by not meaning not to, than by meaning to; that is, from the lack of any good principle rather than from any bad principle which we possess consciously.

The life of Benedict Arnold gives a striking example of the wretched results which may spring from the lack of good principles that are distinctly held.    After telling the story of his treachery, Mr. John Fiske says of him, " In better days he had shown much generosity of nature.   Can it be that this is the same man who, on the field of Saratoga, saved the life of the poor soldier who in honest fight had shot him and broken his leg? Such are the strange contrasts that we sometimes see in characters that are governed by impulse and not by principle.   Their virtue may be real enough while it lasts, but it does not weather the storm." [1]

---

[1] John Fiske's "The American Revolution," vol. II., page 217.

# CHAPTER VIII.

## THE BREAKING UP OF THE ETHICS OF CUSTOM.

WE have seen that in the early history of the world the rules of morality were not distinct from those of custom. There comes a time, however, when the customs of a people are so much disturbed that it is impossible for them to continue to be the only rule of life.

This breaking up occurs in part because *as life becomes complicated, customs come into collision with one another*, so that a man cannot follow one without neglecting another.

It arises in part, also, from the fact that *the people of one community come into relations with those of another*, and find customs different from those to which they have been used.

The condition of such a people is like that of the boy or girl who goes from the home to the school, or from the school into the world, and finds ways of life very different from those that had been familiar. When such a time comes in the history of a people, men are forced to think for themselves instead of blindly following any custom. Some will try to find out what is really right and really wrong. Some will doubt whether there is any right or any wrong.

We have an interesting picture of such a breaking up

of the morality of custom, in the history of Greece. One illustration of this may be found in the life of Socrates.

The Greeks had certain oracles, the utterances of which were recognized as authoritative. Men applied to them, in regard to both public and private matters. They asked whether they should engage in this or that enterprise, and, indeed, sought an answer to any difficult question. Socrates claimed that a divine power directed him in his life, and especially, it would seem, warned him what he should not do. That is, he had a private oracle. Here we have an individual acting independently of the custom. It was, in a sense, the introduction of the right of private judgment among the Greeks. This excited great anger among the people. When, in spite of his goodness, he was put to death, one of the accusations which were brought against him was that he had introduced new divinities. This meant that, so far as his private oracle was concerned, he had acted independently of the custom of the state.

In the Greek tragedies there are very striking pictures of this law of custom.

One of these tragedies, for example, tells the story of Antigone. The king had commanded that no one should perform funeral rites for her brother. To perform such rites for those near to one was considered by the Greeks one of the most sacred duties. Custom also commanded that the king should be obeyed. Antigone could not comply with both these requirements. She was obliged to choose for herself what she should do.

She performed the sacred rites for her brother and suffered the penalty of disobedience to the king.

When the authority of custom was thus breaking up, how could people determine what it was right to do? They could act only as the young man or the young woman does who goes out into a world of maxims and customs that differ from one another and from the maxims and customs of home. They must try to find certain principles, according to which they can live.

## CHAPTER IX.

### THE EPICUREANS.

As Greece, when it was passing from its childhood to its maturity, had to meet the same question which the young man or woman has to meet to-day on going out into the world, it may be helpful to consider one or two of the answers that were given by the Greeks.

The question was, you will understand, "What are the principles according to which life ought to be guided?" Some of the answers given by the Greeks have become very famous.

One of the most famous of these is that which was given by Epicurus. It was that the true principle of living is to get all the happiness that is possible. Men should live to get happiness.

According to this principle, when one questions whether he should or should not perform a certain act, he should ask himself, whether the doing it, or the not doing it, would make him the happier. If it is the telling of a lie, or the taking of something that belongs to another, or the helping one that needs, the question is not, "Is it right?" but, "Will the doing it make me happier or unhappier?"

Epicurus got out of this a better morality than would have seemed possible. He showed that one who does what is right is, on the whole, happier than one who does what is wrong; that temperance brings more happiness than intemperance, virtue than vice, honesty than dishonesty. He thus taught what was practically a lofty morality.

The morality that is based on the desire of happiness has, however, two difficulties.

The first of these difficulties is, that one who lives only to be happy *is really less likely to gain happiness than one who lives for something else.* There is this remarkable thing about happiness: those who make it their chief business to find it are more apt to fail than those who take far less pains about it.

When one thinks of living for happiness the most natural thought is that he wants to live to amuse himself. Now, there is no business that is more exacting and wearisome than that of a mere pleasure-seeker. He has a routine in his life like everybody else, and a routine always tends to become mechanical The word amusement means away from the muses, and implies an escape from the serious business of life When there is no such serious business, amusement loses its special characteristic and much of its charm If a boy were playing games all day, the games would become no more interesting than work.

A second reason why one who lives only for happiness is less likely to find it is that only a part of his life can be lived for pleasure. Few boys, for instance, can play games all the time. Most have to go to school or do some kind of work The boy who cares only to play is bored by all this, and enjoys himself

only on the playground; that is, for only a small part of
the day.   The rest of the time, when he is busied with
his tasks, goes for nothing.   He is simply impatient to
be through with them.   The boy who likes his books
and likes to be helpful at home enjoys himself not
merely when he is playing, but also when he is working.
Thus the boy who cares only to play has a good time
only a small part of the day.   One who cares for other
things has a good time all the day.

A third and more important reason why living for
happiness is likely to fail in the end is, that happiness
for the most part springs from being interested in something outside one's self.   It comes largely from self-forgetfulness, and absorption in something for which one
likes to live.   The mere pleasure-seeker is more shut
up within himself.   His plans all have his self in view.
He thus more rarely escapes from himself into that freedom where happiness is most likely to be found.

In these ways we may illustrate the fact that the mere
pleasure-seeker is not likely to find as much pleasure as
one who seeks for something else.   This is the first
difficulty in the plan of Epicurus.

The second difficulty is, that if you make a person
really feel that pleasure is the great end of life, the
chances are that *he will at once seize the pleasures that
are nearest and easiest.*

Epicurus taught that temperance brings more pleasure than intemperance.   But what if some one had said,
" I know that for me, the happiest life would be to eat,
drink, and be merry."   He taught that there is more

happiness in honesty than in dishonesty; but what if some one had said, "For myself, I know that this money which I could get by a little trickery would make me much happier than I could be without it." I do not know what he could have said to those who are persuaded that happiness could be best reached by these means.

One who is honest simply because he has been taught that honesty is the best policy, will probably become dishonest when he thinks that honesty will not pay.

The word Epicure is derived from Epicurus. Now, Epicurus would seem not to have been a man such as we call an Epicure. The word, however, shows that the world has felt that the tendency of his teaching would be to make Epicures.

We should all seek happiness, it is true; but we should have for the great object of our lives something larger and better than happiness.

We should not do right, and be kind and helpful, merely because we think that in this way we shall somehow get more happiness for ourselves. We should do right because it is right, and be kind and helpful because we care for those about us.

At the same time we may learn from Epicurus that, so far as we seek happiness, we must seek it in the way of virtue; and that vice, sooner or later, brings unhappiness.

## CHAPTER X.

### THE STOICS.

ANOTHER principle of conduct which was set forth among the Greeks, and which has also become very famous, was taught by the Stoics.

The teaching of the Stoics was that we should let nothing disturb our self-command and the repose of mind that springs from that. *We should always be masters of ourselves.*

Suppose that a man who was very rich has lost all his property. He is perhaps wholly cast down and wretched. The Stoic would say to him, "What have you lost? Your money was not a part of you." So, if one is suffering pain and ready to despair, the Stoic would say, "Will you let the pain of your body disturb the peace of your mind?"

Thus to the Stoic his mind, that is, his self, was a fortress which he would defend against all attacks. He would be lord of himself, no matter what might happen.

According to the Stoics, it should not be the great object of a man to live happily, or even to live at all Our principle should be that while we live we should live wisely and well. It is not important under what circumstances we live, whether we be rich or poor, admired or despised. It is important that we make the best use of our circumstances, whatever they may be.

We may take an example from the stage. It does not matter to a great actor what part he plays, whether it be that of a king or a beggar, but only that he plays his part well. We applaud an actor, not because he wears a crown or lives in splendor, but because, even if he is in rags, he plays his part grandly. In life, we are apt to think of the part we play as though it were the most important thing; and we are apt to judge men from the place they fill, rather than from the way in which they fill it.

Epictetus, a famous Stoic, took an illustration from the game of ball. In playing ball, he tells us, no one contends for the ball itself, as though it were either a good or an evil. Each player thinks only how he may best throw it or catch it. The interest of the game does not lie in the possession of the ball, but in the skill with which the player catches and throws it. He means that the outward things of life have in themselves no value; but that they are to be prized only for the skill with which we use them.

Indeed, it is true that the happiest persons in the world, and the most useful, have not been the richest or the most prosperous. They have been oftener those with whom the world has dealt less kindly, but who have known best how to use whatever came to them.

There were many noble men among the Stoics, especially among the Romans, whose strong and stern natures made them fit subjects for this teaching. There was Epictetus, from whom I have just quoted. He was not born in Rome, though much of his life was passed there.   He began life as a slave, but later he obtained his freedom.   There was, also, Marcus Aurelius, the Emperor, who taught the doctrine of the Stoics.   We can still gain help from the writings of the Emperor, as well as from those of the freedman, Epictetus.   This fact may illustrate the teaching of the Stoics, that circumstances in themselves are of small account.

As we have received from Epicurus the word Epicure, so from the Stoics we have received the word Stoicism, which is used to-day to express a certain kind of character and disposition.

Stoicism is the habit of mind that takes all things calmly, that is calm in peril, and peaceful in the midst of pain and misfortune.

There is a higher morality than that of Stoicism, but Stoicism is something not to be despised   Indeed, every man ought to be a bit of a Stoic, whatever higher virtues he may possess.

A certain amount of Stoicism forms the best basis upon which the higher virtues can rest.   By this I mean that fortitude, courage, patience, and the like, should make the character strong, while love, sympathy, and helpfulness make it beautiful.

We shall now consider some of the Stoical virtues, and also some others which resemble Stoicism in that they relate to the management of one's own life without special reference to the happiness and welfare of others.

# CHAPTER XI.

## FORTITUDE.

THE word Fortitude is most often used to signify the brave bearing of pain or other suffering.

It does not mean insensibility to pain, for some persons whose natures are very sensitive have shown the greatest fortitude. It means a self-command by which one preserves his independence, and does not let the pain of the body too much disturb the peace of the mind.

Fortitude is a virtue of which the Stoics made great account, both in their teaching and in their lives. When the word Stoicism is used to-day, in the more general sense to which I have referred, and without reference to the ancient Stoics, this heroic bearing of pain is what it most often means.

A fine example of this is found in the life of Epictetus, the Stoic. While he was a slave, it is said, his master, one day, was beating him cruelly. Epictetus said calmly, " If you do not look out you will break my leg." Presently, at a still heavier stroke, the bone snapped. " There," said Epictetus, as calmly as before, " I told you you would break it."

Every boy ought to be enough of a Stoic to bear a certain amount of pain without outcry or flinching.

Indeed, boys do show much of this stoicism in their

plays. In base-ball, for instance, or in foot-ball, there is often great suffering, which the looker-on would never suspect unless he saw the blow, or the fall which caused the pain.

This stoicism may be, in part, *the result of a strong will.* The boy is determined not to lose his self-command. He orders his nature to hold out, and not let itself be conquered by this attack.

This self-command really lessens the pain. Never is it so hard as when the will gives up and lets the suffering have it all its own way.

In a winter morning one boy goes crouching with the cold. He will feel it ten times as much as another who puts a brave front upon it, takes a pride in meeting it. The latter is really less cold, for the blood is quickened with the manly will and warms the body to the fingers' ends.

Physicians tell us that in hospitals some patients die simply because they give up to their disease; while others get well, simply because they keep a strong will, and do not surrender. Such power has the mind over the body.

This self-command may be helped *by a proper pride.* It is manly thus to bear what one has to bear.

When a boy gives way too easily to any pain, he is called by his companions a "cry-baby." This word means that he has no manliness. A baby is not expected to have self-command, or any pride that would keep it from crying at any suffering, however slight.

We often see an amusing example of this pride when

a man falls on some slippery place in the street. When he gets up, however much he may be suffering or mortified, he is apt to look about him with a smile, as if he thought it an excellent joke. He does not want people to think that his spirit fell with his body.

This self-command is helped still more by *interest in other things*.

The boy who is wounded in a game is so full of eagerness that this helps him to forget his pain. So, in a battle, the wounded soldier may, till the fight is over, hardly realize his suffering; and even then he may forget it in the triumph of the victory or in the shame of the defeat.

The early Christians were so full of the fervor of religious faith and love, that, in the persecutions under the Romans, they seem hardly to have felt the smart of the flames, or the tearing of the wild beasts.

The self-command that has been spoken of is often shown by turning the thought away from the suffering and fixing it upon something that interests and distracts the mind.

If one would bear the evils of life heroically, it is important that he should learn to interest himself in things outside himself, so that he can occupy his mind, and not be too much troubled by bodily ills.

So if one would help another bear any suffering, he should not merely pity, and condole with him; he should try to interest him in something: perhaps in a book that he reads to him, or in some plan that he discusses with him.

Every person should train himself to bear pain nobly; not by tormenting himself, but by making the least possible fuss about anything that is painful or unpleasant. He will find chances enough for this training in fortitude without making them for himself.

# CHAPTER XII.

## COURAGE.

COURAGE is another of the Stoic virtues, and, like fortitude, is one form of self-command.

As fortitude consists in *bearing manfully* that which is painful or disagreeable, courage consists in *not shrinking* from what is painful or disagreeable.

You know how you would manage with a shying horse. The horse sees something by the roadside that he is unwilling to pass. He wants, if he must go by it at all, to make a great sweep around it; but what he would rather do is to turn around and make off in the opposite direction as fast as he can. But you, whom we suppose to be riding, want to keep on your own course. Then, too, you think the horse should be trained. You want to make him know that what he is afraid of is only a stump, or something quite as harmless. So you press him on, quietly but firmly, till you bring him close up to the object of his fear. Then his fear is all gone, and the next time you pass you will probably have less trouble.

He will learn also to trust you, because he has seen that you are wiser than he; so the next time, he will be likely to approach what he is afraid of, if he finds that you think it is all right.

Do you not think that you are as much worth train-

ing as a horse? Do not you sometimes want to shy
and to baulk? And do you not need then to make
yourself feel the bit and the spur?

Some boys dread to get up on a cold morning. How
they lie till the last possible moment, shivering with
dread, going through in imagination the shock of the
cold air over and over again, and having all the pain of
a dozen starts, before they make the real start.

Or here is a poor little fellow who is suffering with
the toothache. How he dreads to have the wretched
thing out, how he puts off the moment, making all
manner of excuses for the delay. All the while, he has
both the real pain of the tooth and the imagined pain
of the pulling, which is almost always a great deal worse
than that which the dentist really causes

We all have a great many unpleasant things to do in
life, and a great many persons make themselves much
extra and needless pain in such ways as I have described. They lack courage and resolution  So, instead
of doing the thing at once and being through with it,
they multiply the evil over and over again by hesitation
and dread.

Every person should make it a principle to train
himself to quick resolve and action in all these matters.

If there is a hard or unpleasant thing to be done, he
should take pride in facing it at once like a man, just as,
if he were riding, he would take pride in bringing his
horse promptly and quietly up to the dreaded stump.

He should take pride in having himself under command, so that he shall not make life mean and miser-
able by petty shrinking or fear.

So, if it is only getting up on a cold morning, or learning a hard lesson, or doing a bit of disagreeable work, one should form the habit of meeting the thing at once, and of being through with it. In this way, one will have, not merely the sense of relief that the thing is done, but a sense of manhood and self-command, which is one of the pleasantest things in life.

An old farmer used to tell his boys, when they had a tough bit of wood to split, to strike right at the middle of the knot.

It is a good rule for life, to strike right at the heart of any difficulty.

If you have an unpleasant duty to perform, do it promptly and cheerfully. It will be better done, and you will be stronger and happier.

## CHAPTER XIII.

### COURAGE (*continued.*)

THE word courage is most often used to mean the
resolute facing of danger. In this sense it may be
compared with cowardice on the one side, and recklessness on the other.

The coward is one who, in any relation of life, exaggerates the danger. When we think of it, we see that
there is no condition in which we are absolutely safe.
A mad dog might run into this room at this very
moment and bite us all. The house might take fire.
When we go into the street, a runaway horse might
knock us down, or we might meet a person that has the
small-pox.

All these things, and a great many others, might happen; but we know that no one of them is likely to
happen, and so we do not trouble our heads about
them. We take what precautions seem necessary, and
then live as if we were absolutely safe.

The coward is one who, under some circumstances,
sees these unlikely things as if they would probably
happen. Instead of looking at the regular course of
events, he sees only these almost impossible chances.
If he is in a boat, he expects that she will go the bot-
tom; or if in a train, that it will run off the track.

Sometimes such cowardice is constitutional. It is

like a disease. I knew once a very learned and wise man who would never trust himself on a railway train. I have seen him going down to the station, dressed in his best, before the train was to start; and when it had gone, I have seen him going home again. He had actually been afraid to get into the car. A dog would put him into a great panic. People would, of course, laugh a little about it; but they thought none the worse of him, for they saw that his fear was like a disease that he could not help.

No one likes to be thought a coward; for, in the whole history of the world, a coward has been looked upon with great scorn.

This is for two reasons. One is that *cowardice often implies a lack of common sense.* The coward does not see things as they are. That which is so unlikely that we can leave it wholly out of the account, the coward looks upon as sure to happen.

Another reason why the coward is despised is that *he lacks manliness and fortitude.* He not only thinks the evil will be sure to come; he thinks he cannot bear it, if it does. The brave man thinks less of the possibility of the evil; but if the evil does come, he means to bear it like a man.

Recklessness is just the opposite of cowardice. As the coward sees danger where there is, practically speaking, none, the reckless man does not see it where it actually exists.

The reckless boy, after the first cold night, will skate out over the deep water, without thinking whether the ice is strong enough to bear. He will go out in his boat, in a high wind, without calculating the strength of the wind as compared with his own strength and skill.

This in a sense is bravery, but it is not the real bravery. If a child sits playing on the railway track when the train is coming, we do not say, "How brave that child is!" We think that it has not wit enough to know its danger. So, such cases as I have referred to are what we call *fool*-hardiness; that is, they show the courage of a fool, rather than that of a brave man, for in these cases the boy or the man rushes into danger of which he does not dream.

The really brave man does not overlook the danger. He does not let his mind dwell upon it; but if it exists he knows just what it is. He takes, however, two things into the account.

One of these is his own strength and skill. His notion of these is not based upon vanity. He has tried himself, and knows pretty well what he is able to do.

Another thing that he considers, is the occasion of the risk, if there is any. A man who would rush into a burning house simply to show his courage, we should call a fool. When the fireman goes in, perhaps to save a child, he goes knowing all the danger, though he does not stop to think of this; but he feels that it is his duty, and he is willing to risk his own life in the hope of saving that of another. Thus we admire him for his courage as well as for his self-forgetfulness, and his high sense of moral obligation.

•

# CHAPTER XIV.

## HEROISM.

THE persons who are thus brave in a good cause are called heroes. I suppose there has never been a country or a time which had not its heroes.

When we look back at the history of the world, we see how much we owe to these heroes of the past. We owe to them our liberties, and indeed all that makes life really worth having.

There is no reading more interesting and more helpful than the lives and deeds of such heroes. Such reading is helpful, because it makes us feel how grand it is to be heroic, and may make us resolve to catch something of the same spirit.

It would be a great mistake to think that the names of all the heroes are written in history. There have been many heroic lives which have been humble and unknown, but which deserve the admiration of the world just as much as those that have been more famous. They perhaps sometimes deserve our honor more; because those who lived them knew that they should never receive honor from men. After a battle, men celebrate the deeds of the leaders in the fight; but there has been just as much bravery among the privates, whose names are never heard out of their own little circle; and the fortune of the day depended as much upon their courage, as upon the ability of the general in command.

There is one danger in reading these stories of heroic lives. They may sometimes make us feel as if we were also heroes, when, perhaps, there is very little that is heroic in our lives. We think what we would do if some great occasion offered, and it does not occur to us that we are cowards in the little occasions that meet us any day.

A boy, for instance, walks along the street, thinking of the knights, the stories of whose exploits he has been reading. He wishes that he could have lived in these old times, and thinks what a brave knight he would have been, how he would have protected oppressed ladies, and would have fought the cruel and false knights in the face of any odds. As he thinks about all this, he sees a boy tip over the table of a poor apple-woman by the sidewalk, and then run away and jeer at her from a little distance. Now, the boy that was dreaming about the knights-errant pities the poor woman, and would like to stop and help her pick up her apples; but he does not, for he is afraid that he shall be laughed at. He feels very angry with the boy that played the cruel trick on her, and would like to punish him, but he is afraid that the other might prove to be the stronger. So he passes on, and gives no sign of the pity or the anger that he feels. I hope, however, that he does not imagine himself any longer to be a brave knight of the olden time, for he has shown that he is nothing but a sneak and a coward.

From this illustration it will appear that there are a great many opportunities for heroism in the life of an ordinary man, and even of a boy or girl.

It requires, sometimes, a great deal of heroism for a boy to do right, or even not to do wrong, when his companions may make fun of him for it. They may sometimes call him a coward simply because he is so brave, while they are the cowards who go with the majority against their will.

It requires heroism to stand up for one whom others are tormenting because he is weak, or a stranger, or, for some fancied reason, happens to be unpopular.

It sometimes requires heroism to interfere to save some poor animal that is being abused and tormented

Fighting is not generally a good thing; but if a boy fights let it be for some good cause such as I have named; for the protection of the weak and for the safety of the suffering, rather than in a quarrel about some personal matter. Such fighting is in the spirit of the heroes whose deeds we so much admire.

# CHAPTER XV.

### DIFFERENT KINDS OF HEROES.

IF we knew what a man really admires, we might form some guess as to what sort of a man he is, or at least as to what sort of a man he is likely to be. This, of course, applies only to moral qualities; since a very plain person, for example, may admire beauty, and a weak person may admire strength, all the more for not possessing it.

Even so far as moral qualities are concerned, the principle has exceptions which we need not consider .here. There is truth enough in it to show that it is of great importance to consider what are the qualities that we really admire.

An Indian was once looking at some portraits of other Indians. There was one which represented a person of mild and thoughtful character. It was the one which we perhaps should have selected as the most pleasing of them all. But the savage did not like it. That, he thought, was a pretty poor kind of Indian. There was another picture that represented a chief who was stern and fierce; who seemed as if he would shrink from no act of cruelty. This, the Indian, who was himself wholly uncivilized and fresh from the wilderness, thought was an Indian worthy of the name. This admiration showed what he was at heart, and tended to make him more and more like that which he admired.

Because our admirations have so much importance, it is well to consider a little what kind of persons are admired by different people. The world has always admired its heroes. It is worth while, then, to notice that there are different kinds of heroes, some of whom are worthy of admiration and some are not.

Courage, strength, energy, skill, grace, — all these are worthy of admiration, even when they are displayed in sport. So far as they are within the reach of any one, they are worth being imitated as well as admired. They certainly do not represent the highest kind of heroism. They should not be admired to the exclusion of better types; but they may well receive the enthusiastic applause that is sometimes given to them.

There is something that sometimes passes for heroism which is not heroism at all, and which deserves only contempt. This is found in those *who show their strength only at the expense of the weak.* A "bully" is a person who likes to make those who are weaker than himself fear and obey him. The "bully" is sometimes found on the playground as well as in the larger life of the world. There are often some with whom he passes for a hero. He is apt, however, to be a coward. If he were not, he would choose the strong rather than the weak to measure himself against.

There are others who are called heroes, who have really strength and courage; who face real peril bravely, but who *do this that they may win something that does not belong to them.* They rob and oppress and injure.

Among these false heroes are the pirates and banditti

who are the admiration sometimes of boys that have seen very little of real life. Their ideal of a hero is some sort of robber-king.

The stories of wild, free life in which the buccanneer or the pirate figures, may have a certain fascination, but they have this for us only when we look at them from the outside. I mean that it is when we consider the courage and the craft, and forget those who are robbed or slain.

If a man should creep into your house, should steal whatever he could lay his hands on, should perhaps kill some member of the household, should brave the police, and should escape with his booty, he would have shown courage and skill; but I think you would hardly admire him, even if he gave a part of his plunder to the poor  Now the pirate or the bandit is only the same mean thief dressed up in gayer clothes, and surrounded by more picturesque associations. He is like a carrion bird dressed out in gay plumage. We may admire the plumage; but we can have only disgust for the poor figure that is left, when the feathers are torn away.

We may learn how much the qualities of daring and of adroitness are really worth, when we see them admired and perhaps cannot quite help admiring them ourselves, even in such wretched associations as we have just considered.

Of very much the same stamp are many of those whom the world admires. I mean *the great conquerors* who have sought to win glory and power and even

wealth for themselves, without regard to the happiness
or to the rights of others.   Many of the heroes that the
world honors are thus no better than the buccanneer or
the bandit that  the schoolboy has taken for his hero.

In such cases we may admire the powers which are
shown by the world's conqueror; but these must not
blind us to the real nature of his deeds.   He has finer
feathers than the bandit king, but is, at heart, the same
mean and selfish being.

What is meaner than for one man to cause the death
of thousands, to take away all the joy of countless
homes, simply that the world  may say what a great
man he is, and bow down before him?

It is a great lesson which the world has been slow to
learn, to find that meanness and selfishness are always
the same, no matter how fine a dress they wear, or how
many unite to shout their praise.

How different is military glory *when it is won in the*
*defence of one's country, or in that of the oppressed,* from
what it is when it is sought merely for its own sake.   I
think that the world will sometime outgrow its admiration for the glory that is won for selfish ends alone, but
it will never outgrow its reverence for patriotism and a
chivalry that is impatient of any wrong which is inflicted
upon the weak.

There is no kind of service to mankind that has not
had its heroes.   There have been heroes for truth, for
justice, for philanthropy.

There could be no heroism more worthy of honor
than that of Dorothea Dix, who devoted her life to the

relief of the terrible suffering of the insane in this country. · She was a woman with delicate health and, at first,
without money or prominent friends; yet she caused
a revolution in the treatment of the insane.

You have no idea to what cruelty the insane had
been exposed. They had been kept in filth, without
fire or comfort of any kind. This neglect was not because people were so cruel; it was simply because they
thought that this was the way to treat the insane.

Miss Dix, moved by her intense pity, used all her
great energy and good sense, travelled from state to
state, and from country to country, aroused interest in
others, and guided the interest which she had aroused.
New hospitals were built, wiser and tenderer care was
used, better methods were introduced; so that now we
can hardly believe that things ever were so bad as they
were before her day.[1]

I will mention another hero who was very different,
but who showed his heroism also in reference to the
insane.

Charles Lamb was a writer of charming essays,[2] full
of wit and fancy. He seemed to the world as far as
possible from a hero; yet his life was heroic. He was
engaged to be married to a woman whom he tenderly
loved; but his sister became insane and killed their
mother, and he gave up all his plans, and lived for her.
He undertook to take care of her. She lived with him;
only when her attacks of insanity returned, he took her

---

[1] See the Life of Dorothea Dix, by Francis Tiffany.
[2] The Essays of Elia.

to a hospital till she had recovered. It was a sad sight to see the brother and sister walking across the fields to the hospital together, when she felt that the trouble was coming on. His life was lived for this sister, so sweet and lovely when she was herself, so wild and ungovernable when her fits of insanity came upon her; who in her insanity had committed that terrible deed. This was, you must remember, while the insane, in general, were treated with the cruelty that I have described

I have in mind many heroes of all kinds, to whose lives I should gladly refer, but I have no space. They are found in all forms of life. There are railway engineers, who, when they saw that a collision could not be avoided, have remained at their place to lighten, if possible, the shock, and have been killed; sea captains, who have remained at their posts till all others had left, and have gone down with their ships, physicians and nurses, and sisters of charity, who have not shrunk from pestilence in order to save life, or to comfort the dying. There was Father Damien, a catholic priest, who so pitied the lepers, who were confined to an island, deprived alike of the comforts of this world and of the consolation of religion, that he went to live with them. He knew that when he once joined them he should probably take their disease, and, in any case, could never leave them. But he went to them and shared their lot, living and dying with them, seeking to do them good.

I would advise each of you to keep a book of heroes, and put down in it the names of all the heroic persons

of whom you read in history, or in the newspapers, or
of whom you hear in your daily life. You can make
divisions and classes of heroes, according to the purpose
of their acts, whether for patriotism, or science, or philanthropy, or religion, or whatever cause. Then you
can decide who are the greatest heroes, and whom you
would rather be like. Only remember that keeping a
book of heroes is not to be heroic; seek really to be a
hero in your own life.

There are many who have been heroes in the most
common lives; boys and girls who have sacrificed many
pleasures to obtain an education; boys and girls who
have given up the idea of an education, because they
felt that they were too much needed by their parents or
by their younger brothers or sisters; those who have
given up the dearest plans, or the most attractive pleasures, for the sake of those who were dependent upon
them. It is as heroic to give up one's pleasure for the
sake of the sick at home, as to go to serve in a hospital.
Heroism needs no setting-off of romance to be worthy
of the name.

Such unpretending heroes as I have described are
worthy to have their names in your hero-book; and to
be imitated in your lives.

# CHAPTER XVI.

## CONTENTMENT.

FOR contentment are needed both the fortitude and the courage of which we have been speaking: fortitude to bear cheerfully whatever may be disagreeable in the present; and courage to meet bravely the uncertainties of the future.

The habit of discontent is something like cowardice. As cowardice sees all possible elements of danger, but does not see the elements of safety which far outbalance the others, so discontent sees only what is unpleasant, and overlooks the mass of pleasant things which for the most part outnumber them.

As there is always, theoretically speaking, some vague and remote possibility of the perils that cowardice fears, so discontent is never wholly without reason. In every life there are actually some things which are not agreeable. Discontent sees them and thus justifies itself. Its mistake is that it sees these alone, or out of all proportion with other things.

If you are discontented, the feeling is probably based upon something which is really unpleasant, and you may, in thinking upon this, feel that your discontent is justified. What you have to consider, however, is whether this bit of discomfort is not outweighed by pleasant things, and whether you are right in letting this take away the comfort of your life.  There is rather a slangy proverb which has a good deal of common sense in it.  It says of something that one does not fancy, " If you do not like it, you must lump it."  That is, you must not take it by itself, but let it find its place in the whole of your life.

There is a story of a man who determined that one person in the world should be perfectly happy.  He found a poor woman living most wretchedly, took her out of her wretchedness, gave her a nice little cottage, with a pleasant garden, and clothing and money and all that seemed needed for her comfort.  In a year he came to see her to hear the story of her happiness, but he found her as wretched as ever.  Her neighbor had a pea-hen, the voice of which was so unpleasant to her that it took away all her pleasure, and she was as unhappy as she was at first.  This woman was perfectly right in not liking the voice of the pea-hen, which is certainly not musical; but she was wrong in letting this single bit of unpleasantness take away her satisfaction in all the pleasant things that were around her.

It might be thought that the habit of discontent would bring its own cure.  Certainly it brings its own punishment.  We often try to correct faults by showing the unhappiness that they will bring; but the habit of discontent, by its very nature, brings unhappiness, so that the connection between the two does not need to be pointed out.

It is as if at a table there were several dishes of sweet and pleasant food, and one of food that is bitter to the taste; and a person should take of the bitter food and mingle it with all the rest, so that nothing should be agreeable, and should then complain of the bitterness of all. So the habit of discontent spoils the more abundant good, by spreading over it the less abundant evil.

Strange as it may seem, however, the habit of discontent brings certain satisfactions with it.

One of these is that it is associated with *a certain feeling of superiority*. The discontented person often thinks that great dissatisfaction with that to which other persons submit quietly, shows a greater delicacy of nature than these others possess.

Hans Christian Andersen tells a story of a queen who wished her son to marry only a true princess; so she devised a test by which the true princess should be known. She piled on the bedstead half a dozen beds, and under the lowest of these she placed a rose-leaf. She made one and another, for whom the hand of the prince was sought, sleep on the bed thus prepared. When they came down in the morning and said that they had slept beautifully, her thought was, "Ah, you are not a true princess." At last, one came down in the morning saying that she had had a fearful night, and was all black and blue; for there was something hard in the bed which took away all her peace. She had felt the rose-leaf under all the feathers that buried it; and by this the queen recognized the true princess.

There are those who think that to be troubled by every little annoyance shows their superiority, as if they were true princes and princesses. They might as well be proud of a poor digestion, or of a lame leg.

The habit of discontent has another satisfaction some-what similar to this.   The dissatisfied person has enjoy-ment *in thinking that his surroundings are very far below his deserts.*   He has such a sense of his own im-portance that he feels injured by anything that is not quite to his satisfaction, and this sense of injury increases the sense of personal importance.

This kind of discontent may perhaps be lessened if the discontented person should really ask himself how it is that he has deserved so much; what he is or what he has done, by which he can claim to have only pleasant things in the world, while so many have so much suffering.

It may be helpful to think of others, good and true, who cheerfully bear evils, compared with which those that cause the discontent are as nothing.

The habit of discontent arises, in general, from *the mistake of supposing that any arrangement of outward things can in itself make us happy.*   Certainly, it is eas-ier to be happier in some circumstances than in others; but none in themselves can bring happiness.

Every one should learn the art of living, and this art consists in being able to use the circumstances of life, and not to be at their mercy; to live cheerfully even when everything is not precisely as one would have it.

You have seen the pretty wood carvings that are made in Switzerland.   You would be surprised to find with how simple an apparatus they are made.   You go into the workshop and expect to find a great array of tools. You find, perhaps, a young man with nothing but a piece of wood and a jack-knife. So out of the simplest materials, and with the poorest tools, many have carved beautiful lives which have been a joy to themselves and those about them.

But, after all, this is very much a matter of habit. We see what we look for, and what we are in the habit of seeing. One used to correcting proof, for instance, will see at a glance a page disfigured by typographical errors that another would never notice; simply because he has made it his habit to look for them.

So, one that has formed the habit of seeing unpleasant things will see them and perhaps will see little else, while one in the habit of paying more attention to what is pleasant than to what is unpleasant will find what is pleasant at almost every turn.

There are few things that are more important for the happiness of life than to form a habit of taking a cheerful view of the circumstances in which one is placed.

## CHAPTER XVII.

### AMBITION.

THE habit of contentment which we have been considering may, in some respects, be carried too far. One may be too contented. While we should make the best of things that cannot be changed, and not let our lives be poisoned by discontent, it is a mistake and even a fault to be satisfied with what can without loss or injury be made better.

This sort of contentment sometimes takes the form of shiftlessness. We sometimes pass a house in the country where the gates are off the hinges, the fences are broken, the grounds are full of weeds, when a little labor would make all these things right. We think that the man who lives there takes things too easily. He is too contented. He needs a little dissatisfaction to spur him on.

The habit of mind that seeks to excel is called ambition.

Ambition may be a very good or a very bad thing, according to its object. As it is the powder in the gun that sends the ball whizzing on its way for good or for evil, so it is ambition that gives energy and movement to the life. It is as important to have ambition directed rightly as it is to have a loaded gun pointed in the right way; but a life without ambition is of little more use than a gun without powder

A true ambition may be directed to *improving the circumstances of one's life.* It is a good ambition for a
poor boy to think that he will work hard, and will some
day have a comfortable home for himself and those
whom he loves. Even the ambition to be rich is often
a worthy one; only it must be remembered that riches
may be purchased at too dear a price.

It is a worthy ambition *to do well whatever one does.*
This is an ambition which nobody should be without.
Even in the play-ground one should have an ambition
to play well, to be a good pitcher or catcher, or to excel
in whatever part one has to play. A boy who is care-
less and indifferent in a game of ball will not be likely to
accomplish much anywhere.

We like to see even a horse ambitious, and not moving only as fast as the whip forces it. We like to see a
workman ambitious to turn out good work, whether it
be a stone wall that he is building, or shoes that he is
making. We like to see a scholar ambitious to take a
good place in his class, and to have his lesson perfectly.

This sort of ambition makes play even of the hardest
work, for it puts life into everything that one does;
while the lack of ambition will make work even of play, for
if one has no interest to do well what one is doing, then
even base-ball is little better than a task.

Above all, one should be ambitious *to do the best
things.*

There are all sorts of ambitions in life. We laugh at
the small boy the height of whose ambition is to strut
through the street with a cigarette in his mouth. We

despise the young man whose ambition is to be a little faster than his fellows. We have also a contempt for the man who is simply trying to get rich while he cares nothing for the good opinion of his fellow citizens, nothing for honesty or honor, or for the needs of those that he can help.

We admire the ambition of one who means to be a manly man, to be a kindly friend, to get on in the world himself and to help others get on in it; who, in a word, means to be an honorable and useful citizen, and to make the world better and happier.

## CHAPTER XVIII.

### EDUCATION AS A DUTY.

WE have seen that the ambition to make the most and the best of one's self is worthy of all praise. One of the most important helps in accomplishing this end is education. To obtain an education so far as is possible is thus one of the first duties which one owes to one's self.

By education, I mean the teaching which one may receive at home, at school, at college or elsewhere, and also that which one may give to one's self.

Boys and girls go to school, — some because they have to, and some as a mere matter of course. Perhaps very few ask themselves what is the real good of going to school. This I will now try to explain.

Men differ from the lower animals, in part, because whatever one generation of men gains is passed on to the next, so that each starts with some little advantage over the one that went before it

Each generation of animals, so far as we now know them, starts just where the former generation started

That is, each generation of birds builds its nests in the same way in which birds of its kind have built them, so far as we know anything about them. So the bees make honey and the beavers make dams just as their parents and grand-parents have done for centuries.

There was probably a time in the past when the present skill was reached by slow and hardly perceptible advance; but so far as our definite knowledge goes, there has been little, if any, change from generation to generation.

There is, also, this difference between man and the lower animals, that what man does he has to learn how to do, while the animals are able to do the most that they accomplish by what we call instinct; that is, without having to learn how.

Some things, indeed, that seem most natural to them, the animals have to learn. Thus the birds would not sing unless they heard other birds sing. If a bird is brought up with birds of a different kind, it will often sing their song instead of that which belongs to it. Thus the canary has to be put, as we might say, to school to an older canary that is a good singer, or it could not sing any more than a child that has never been taught. But most things that the animals do, they do without teaching. I suppose the bees would make honey, and the birds would build their nests, and the beavers would make dams, even if they had never seen these things done by their parents.

You can now see why boys and girls should go to school.

It is *in order that they may get the best experience of all the generations that have gone before*, and may make a fair start with the one that is just beginning. A boy or girl who is not taught the most important of these results of past ages, might just as well have been born

hundreds of years ago in a savage hut.   The boy or girl
who is unwilling to be taught is trying to throw away the
advantage of living to-day, and is really seeking to have
no better start in life than a savage boy or girl could
have that was born hundreds of years ago.

I have said that the boy or the girl is taught the most
important results of all the experience of the past   Of
course it is very little that can be thus taught.   We are,
as the poet Tennyson says, "the heirs of all the ages."[1]
but all that the child or the youth can be taught is how
to get all these great possessions.

Think what a gain it is simply to be able to read, and
to read intelligently, and to love to read   As soon as
one has accomplished this, all the treasures of the
knowledge and the thought of the past are open to him.
It is as if the key of a great treasure-house were put
into his hand and he were told to go and help himself
to whatever he would have.

The same is true of whatever else is taught at school.
Each study well pursued puts a key into the hand of the
scholar, by which he may unlock one of the doors of
the world, which would otherwise be closed to him.

But after all, the mind itself is the best tool; and
the best thing that the scholar learns at school is to use
his mind.

[1]   In Locksley Hall.

## CHAPTER XIX.

### SELF-EDUCATION AS A DUTY.

WE hear, often, of self-educated men. By these words are meant men who had little advantage of instruction in early life, but who, by making the most of themselves and of the opportunities they had, have reached, often, positions of great honor and usefulness. In our country we have had many such men, of whom President Lincoln may serve as a striking example.

But, in fact, all men who amount to anything are in a sense self-made men. The best teachers in the world cannot make a youth amount to anything, unless he takes the matter into his own hands, and works with them.

In the power to train himself, man differs from most lower animals. You have to train a horse. The horse does very little towards his own training, except to be docile in the hands of his master. Some animals, indeed, do very much more than this and try to train themselves. An elephant is sometimes found practising by himself the lessons he has been taught; and a parrot will drill itself, trying to get the words which its owner wants to teach it. These are, however, exceptional cases.

Self-education lies outside the school-room as well as in it. There is no part of the nature which one ought not to try to educate.

*The body should be educated.* The limbs should be made strong and supple. Most of us do not know even how to stand or to walk. See a civilian stand or walk by the side of a soldier, and how crooked and lumpish he almost always appears. The soldier has learned how to carry himself; the civilian has not. Out-of-door games do much for such training,—rowing and running and ball and the rest. Then there is the gymnasium which develops the form regularly and gives the man the mastery of himself.

*The senses should be trained to sharpness and accuracy.* Now and then, by way of advertisement, a prize is offered to the person who guesses most nearly the amount held by a big teapot, or some other vessel of the same sort. People guess wildly and for the most part have no idea what the amount should be. Something like this, in a systematic way, would be good training for every one.

A boy should not think that he has learned the tables of weights and measures till he has some idea what the words really mean. He should be able to tell whether the weight that he holds is a pound, whether the space that he marks off is a foot.

You could easily make a game out of such training, with prizes or whatever else would give interest to it. Who can tell most correctly how many acres there are in such a field, or when he has walked a mile? All this should be tried till it is no longer mere guessing, but one knows something of what he is talking about.

Then, too, *the senses should be trained to observe.*

How many go through the world without seeing anything accurately! I have already suggested that it is a good plan to study some science, so that one will get into the habit of noticing what is before him.

*The hands, too, should be trained to skill.* It is a great thing to have the mastery of tools. If one has only a jack-knife, it is a great thing to be able to make something definite with it, and not merely to whittle a stick into nothing but whittlings.

*It is still more important to cultivate the mind.* Anybody who can read can do this. I shall speak of this again later, so I will not dwell upon it now.

One should not be afraid to seek information and help from the older persons that one is with. Especially in the school, one should consider the teacher as a friend, who is ready and eager to help, and whose business it is to help.

There is another matter that we may often forget, and that is *the training of the feelings.* One who is lazy, or quarrelsome, or selfish, ought to try very hard to make something different of himself.

In a word, you should consider what sort of a man you would like to be. Think of those you have known, or those of whom you have read or heard, and when you make up your mind what sort of a man you would like to be, take yourself in hand, and try to make of yourself such a person. Treat yourself as if you were somebody else that you had charge of, and see what a good training-master you can be.

# CHAPTER XX

## SELF—RESPECT.

SELF—RESPECT is the foundation of all true manliness and womanliness. When a person has lost this, there is little that can be done for him.

Self-respect is largely the basis of the virtues that we have been considering. Ambition, courage, fortitude, and other forms of self-control, imply that a person has such respect for himself that he likes to fill his place well, and to hold his own in the world. It is because the coward lacks self-respect that he is willing to flee. It is self-respect that inspires fortitude, and prevents one from ignominiously collapsing in the presence of what is painful or unpleasant.

Self-respect is a great help in meeting and bearing whatever mortifies our vanity, or tempts to envy and jealousy.

*Vanity* finds its delight solely in the good opinion of others; *Self-respect* is, to a great degree, independent of the opinion of others.

We should, up to a certain point, seek the good opinion of those about us; and it is natural to enjoy the possession of it. Self-respect, however, will not stoop to any meanness to gain it, and though the person who respects himself may be troubled when this good opinion is lost without good cause, he will not fret too much about it. *for* (There is something that is to him more important than the good-will of others; that is his respect for himself. )

It is well to remember that there is no unfailing recipe against trouble in the world. The good person is not always happy. Even religion does not undertake to make men perfectly happy in the world. It helps them to bear trouble, and to get some higher good out of it. Such help implies that there is still trouble to be borne

Thus the self-respecting person may be pained by dislike and neglect; but he will not feel them as a person does whose only support is in the good opinion of other people.

Self-respect is a great help against *envy and jealousy.* How much there is to provoke to jealousy, even among young people at school. One scholar stands higher in the class; another has finer clothes; another is more popular among the other scholars.

An envious or jealous person will find in all this the source of great unhappiness. He will perhaps hate his rival who is preferred, and hate the teacher or the companions who give the preference. He will perhaps become discouraged or ill-tempered.

Instead of trying to tell you how a self-respecting boy or girl would meet all this, I will tell you how a self-respecting boy did meet it.

One of the most brilliant writers of France has published a book, which is, he tells us, in its first part, the story of his own life.[1]   The hero of the story, in whom

---

[1] "Le petit Chose," by Alphonse Daudet.

the author represents himself, is a poor boy, who lived in the city of Lyons, in France. He obtained an opportunity to attend, without expense, a school made up mostly of boys from rich families. He went wearing a blouse, such as is often worn by the poorer men and boys in France. When he entered the school-room, his first glance showed that his was the only blouse there. He saw the boys tittering, and from every side he heard whispered, "He has come in a blouse!" As days went on, even the master was mean enough to take part against him because he was poor  The master never called him by his name. When he spoke to him it was, "Come here, What's-your-name," or, "What are you about, What's-your-name?" Another boy might, as I have said, have become discouraged, envious, jealous, and very unhappy  But see what this boy, who respected himself, did. He said to himself, "If I am to take any position in this school *I must work twice as hard as the other boys.*" This he did. Later, when he was a great man, we may imagine with what pleasure and pride he placed, as the title of the book which was the story of his life, the words which the master had so often addressed to him in contempt. This title we may translate freely into "Little What's-his-name."

A person who respects himself will not stoop to what is mean or dishonorable. If his sense of duty is not strong enough to preserve him from such things, his self-respect will keep him from them. He will be ashamed to do a dishonorable thing.

We can now compare, better than we could have done before, self-respect with pride.

Self-respect is a kind of pride. It is the good pride. The bad pride is that which compares one's self with others, and looks down upon them.

Pride differs from vanity, in that the proud man has such contempt of others that he does not care very much what they think of him.

When I was a very small boy, a lady was talking with me about " easily besetting sins." She said that her besetting sin was pride. I looked at her in innocent wonder and exclaimed, "Why, what have you to be proud of?" I saw at once by her confusion that I had made a very impudent and unlucky speech. We cannot ask this question of others; but if anyone who is disposed to be proud should ask himself the question, " What have you to be proud of?" and answer it truly, it might do him good.

Self-respect is a pride that makes no comparison with others. The man who respects himself is simply ashamed to do anything that would be unworthy of him.

He respects himself as he would have others respect him. One who does not respect himself cannot expect to be respected by others.

# CHAPTER XXI.

## SELF-RESPECT (*continued*).

RESPECT for one's self is shown in many ways besides those that have been mentioned. It is seen, for instance, in neatness or cleanliness.

It is pleasant to see a young woman, however poor she may be, never forgetting to keep herself clean and neat. Even a little personal adornment, however simple, shows that, in spite of difficult circumstances, she has not lost her self-respect.

It is unpleasant to see a dirty child, although it is not the child's fault. You can see, however, from the disgust that you have in seeing a dirty child, how disgusting a filthy person always is.

Even most animals like to keep clean. We are sometimes disgusted with the filth in which the hog lives; but that is not its fault, but its owner's. Even a hog would keep clean if it could. I knew of one that had a sleeping-room in the barn, from which an opening led into a little yard outside. This yard was like other pig-sties, but the sleeping-room was kept perfectly neat. The straw which was given it for a bed, it cut up with its teeth so that it was fine and soft. All this it kept swept, I do not know how, neatly in a corner, where it could lie with its nose at the opening so as to get the freshest air possible. When I see pigs living in filth, I think of this one and pity them; for I know that they would be neat if they could. From this it appears that a person who does not like to keep clean is worse even than a pig.

While the hog, from the way in which men make him live, stands, in spite of himself, as an illustration of the disgusting nature of filthiness, the cat may serve as an example of personal cleanliness. How the cat likes to wash herself with her tongue! A poor way, we should think; but it is her only way, of keeping clean.

A cat was not well and needed medicine. She refused to take it, just as some children do. She had, however, a better excuse than they, for no one could tell her that it was for her good. She did not like it, and saw no reason why she should take it. A bright girl, fresh from Ireland, exclaimed, "Give me some grease and I will make her take it!" She mixed the medicine with the grease, and smouched it over the cat's fur. The cat disliked the taste, but she disliked more to have her fur soiled, so she licked it all off, and was cured in spite of herself.

Neatness and cleanliness, by showing the self-respect of the person who is neat and clean, go far to win for him the respect of others. When a young man or woman seeks a position of any kind, there is hardly anything that could harm the chance of success more than an untidy and uncleanly appearance.

A self-respecting person should be ashamed to live in an uncleanly or untidy house.

Cleanliness here has also its practical side. Typhoid

fever, and other terrible diseases, are caused, as we now know, by little living things, far too small to be seen except with the help of the microscope, that get into the body and work these evils. These little beings are bred to a large extent in filth. We see this illustrated on a large scale by the fact that when a pestilence visits a community, it is the lack of cleanliness in certain localities that does the most to invite it, and to stimulate its ravages.

Much worse than outward filth is inward impurity. No person with any self-respect would stoop to this. Impure thoughts are far more disgusting than unclean face and hands.

How would a person who encourages impure thoughts feel if his mind were suddenly thrown open to the world, so that all could see them? One should never do or think what he would be ashamed to have those about him know.

Indeed, the exposure that was suggested in the last paragraph takes place up to a certain degree. One who is given to this kind of thought tends to show the effect of it, at last, in his face. He thinks that nobody suspects; but those who have insight and delicate feeling see what the condition of his mind is, and have a loathing such as few other things can cause.

There are many other things which a feeling of self-respect leads one to avoid. Indeed it is the enemy of all the vices and the encourager of all the virtues, as it is the heart and soul of manliness.

## CHAPTER XXII.

### SELF-CONTROL.

ONE of the most important lessons which one has to learn is that of self-control.

The person who is without self-control does at every moment just what he feels like doing. He will speak the words that come into his mind, no matter how cruel or unkind they may be. He will eat what he feels like eating, and drink what he feels like drinking, no matter how harmful the thing is.

He is like anything else that is untrained; like a troublesome child, or a dog that has never learned to mind. Only in this case it is himself that the person has never taught to obey.

It is worth while, sometimes, to keep from doing something that is not harmful, but very tempting, simply to see that one has this mastery of one's self: just as we forbid a dog that we are training to do this or that; not that there is any harm in the thing, but so that he may learn to mind our word.

I have seen a dog sit up with a piece of meat on his nose, and make no motion to eat it until the word of command was given. Such a dog is in fine training. We ought to have the same mastery over ourselves that the owner has over his dog. One who has not this mastery is at the mercy of anything. He is like one who is driving a horse that is not well broken. At the critical moment the horse may start, and dart to one side, or run, and he who seems to be the driver, because he holds the reins, may be dashed to the ground.

Long ages ago, in both Greece and India, philosophers compared the senses to horses well or ill-trained, and the comparison may be helpful to us now.

The habit of eating everything that comes in one's way if it tempts the taste, and of eating too much, is called gluttony. This often does much to destroy the health; as well as, by the habit of greediness, to prepare one for all kinds of loathsome vices when one is older.

Still more dangerous is the habit of drinking whatever tempts the taste. This, when what is so drunk is intoxicating liquor, is called intemperance.

Intemperance is one of the most contemptible and loathsome habits into which one may fall. It is also one of the most dangerous. It springs from the lack of self-control, and it destroys what little self-control may still exist.

A person who "drinks" gives up all self-command. He is like a man who, in the midst of a perilous region, throws the reins over his horse's back and lets him take what course he will. The best tempered man, when he has drunk too much, may become quarrelsome, the kindest hearted one may become brutal and cruel, the most sensible one may become a fool, and all become alike ridiculous.

One great peril about this matter of drink is that one who indulges in it *may reach a point where he has no mastery of himself.* He may think that he will take a glass now and then and be none the worse. He does it because a friend offers it, or because he thinks he must treat a friend, or because others do, or because he is beginning to like it; and, all at once, before he has dreamed that it was possible, the drunkard's thirst may be kindled, before which he feels himself powerless.

I suppose that there is nothing more terrible than the drunkard's thirst. It is stronger than his love for his parents or his wife or his children, stronger than his love of respectability, stronger than his dread of poverty or ridicule. It is a burning thirst, terrible in its torment and never to be satisfied in its demands.

In some, this thirst is kindled much more easily than in others, but there are none who are wholly free from the peril of it, and no one can tell in advance how soon his turn may come. He may laugh at another who has fallen, but at the next moment he may find himself at the mercy of this raging demon.

Far above the falls of Niagara, one may row down the river and turn back when he will. But as he goes down further, there comes a point beyond which he cannot turn back. The trouble is that he can never know when he is reaching that point. He thinks that he is safe and will turn back; but the stream has him in its power, and hurries him on, down towards the terrible plunge of the cataract. So it is when one begins to drink intoxicating liquor. He cannot tell in advance when the point is reached beyond which he is helpless.

I do not say that it is ever too late for the drunkard

to reform but, if he does, it may be at the cost of a struggle more terrible than we can conceive, and in which few have the strength and the resolution to win.

For boys and young men, at least, who are exposed to temptation, and all boys and young men are liable to be so exposed, the only safe way is to taste nothing that will intoxicate. In this way one is safe. But if one takes such drink, however rarely at first, he may find himself drawn into the deadly current.

One may laugh at this peril, but it is like laughing at the danger from some contagious disease. One may say in his pride of health, "I am safe," and the next moment the disease may have taken possession of his body.

# CHAPTER XXIII.

### SELF—RELIANCE.

IT is important to learn early to rely upon yourself, for little has been done in the world by those who are always looking out for some one to help them.

We must be on our guard not to confound self-reliance with self-conceit, yet the difference between the two cannot easily be defined in words.

The difference is something like that between bravery and foolhardiness, which was spoken of in an earlier chapter.[1]

The self-conceited person takes it for granted that he is superior to others. The self-conceited girl thinks that she is handsomer, more graceful, or more talented, than other girls, that her work is nicer, or that her composition shows more genius. Whatever is to be done, she thinks that she can do it better than another, and that her way is always the best. The self-conceited boy looks upon himself and his exploits in the same way. It is hard to correct self-conceit, because all that such self-satisfied persons do seems to them so nearly perfect that they are liable to grow more and more conceited.

It is one advantage of going to school that girls and boys are apt to have the conceit more or less taken out of them, because they are often thrown among others

---

[1] See chapter XII,

who are superior to them, and because their companions have little patience with such pretence.

Self-reliance is very different from self-conceit. The self-reliant person is often very modest. He does not say about anything that is to be done, "I am so strong and wise that I can do it." He says, "I will try, and if patience and hard work will do it, it shall be done."

One way in which a person may become self-reliant, is never to seek or accept help till he has fairly tried what can be done without it.

Some scholars, if they come to a problem that seems hard, run at once to the teacher, or an older friend, or perhaps even to another scholar, who is brighter or more self-reliant than themselves, in order to be told how to do it. Always try it yourself. Even if it is nothing more important than a conundrum, do not wish somebody to tell you the answer till you have fairly tried to conquer it.

It is a pleasant feeling that comes from having done a difficult thing one's self, a feeling that those never have who are helped out of every hard place.

It is like the feeling that one has after having climbed a steep mountain. There is a healthy pride in having conquered the difficulty of the ascent. There is also the comfortable feeling that comes when the muscles have been used without being unduly strained. There is a similar pleasant sensation when the mind has been exerted successfully, in learning, for instance, a difficult task, or solving a hard problem.

One who has overcome one difficulty is ready to

meet the next with confidence that it, too, will yield to his attempt.

See how, much such a person has gained. In later life, while others are hesitating what to do, or whether to do anything, he goes forward and accomplishes what he undertakes.

It is often better to do a thing by a way that is not the very best than not to do it at all.

Self-reliance is as important in *thought* as it is in action.

Some people find it hard to make up their minds. They run to one and another to get advice. Perhaps it is in regard to nothing more important than the color of a dress. Perhaps the bits of advice which they receive conflict with one another; then such people are worse off than they were before.

No person knows better the real value of advice than he who is self-reliant. He has measured his own powers so often that he knows where he needs help.

When advice comes from those who have wisdom and experience, it is to be taken thankfully.

So far as people in general are concerned, it is often hard for them to put themselves into your place sufficiently to give the advice that you really need. The very fact of having to do a thing often suggests the best way of doing it. Your own thought in regard to anything that you have to do, is thus often better than that of the companion whose advice you seek.

It is pleasant, and sometimes helpful, to talk over our plans with a friend; but we must remember that it is we ourselves who must make the decision.

Did you ever think why it is that so many of the great men of our country are found among those who began life in hardship and poverty? Many of them grew up in what was, when they were young, the western frontier, where they had to work hard; where they had no schools, and few comforts and conveniences. They have come from circumstances that seemed wholly discouraging, and have become presidents, judges, generals, or millionaires.

You would find it interesting to put down the names of those that have reached such success from such hard beginnings, and keep a list of them. If you are careful to learn about such persons, and to write down their names, you will be astonished to see how long your list will become. Such a list you could keep as a special division in the book of heroes of which I have spoken in another place.[1]

Many who were thus situated in their youth did not reach such prominent positions. They became often, however, enterprising and useful citizens. They will not be added to your list, but they lived no less successful, and perhaps happier, lives than those whose names have become familiar to the world. One reason why so many that had such an unpromising beginning have won great success is, that because they had so few helps they were forced to help themselves. They thus became self-reliant. When they went out into the world they went straight ahead. Without waiting for any one to

---

[1] See page 51.

make a place for them, they made a place for themselves. Without waiting for any one to do for them,
they did for themselves. Without waiting for people to
advise them, they trusted themselves. They were
prompt, energetic and sensible. Thus people trusted
them and honored them.

Though you have the helps that such men were
forced to do without, yet you can cultivate the habit
of self-reliance. You can solve your own problems, do
your own tasks, and meet your own difficulties, and
thus you, too, can be preparing to do your own part in
the world.

When I was a young man, I was with a friend on the
shore of a lake in the Maine woods. We wanted to
fish; we found a boy, perhaps ten years old, who got a
boat for us, showed us where the best place to fish was,
pulled with us out on the lake, and made himself very
serviceable. When we had finished, we offered him
some money for the boat and his help. He refused to
take it. He straightened himself up and said, "I
wanted to fish myself"

I have often thought of that manly boy, self-reliant
and contented with himself. He did not want favors
that he did not need from strangers whom he did not
know.

All this reminds me of a fable which I read when I was
a boy, and which I have remembered ever since: —
Some larks had a nest in a field of grain. One evening
the old larks coming home found the young ones in
great terror. "We must leave our nest at once," they

cried. Then they related how they had heard the farmer say that he must get his neighbors to come the next day to help him reap his field. "Oh!" cried the old birds, "If that is all, we may rest quietly in our nest." The next evening the young birds were found again in a state of terror. The farmer, it seems, was angry because his neighbors had not come, and had said that he should get his relatives to come the next day and help him. The old birds took the news easily, and said there was nothing to fear yet. The next evening the young birds were very cheerful. "Have you heard nothing to-day?" asked the old ones. "Nothing important," answered the young. "It is only that the farmer was again angry because his relatives also had failed him, and he said to his sons, 'Since neither our neighbors nor our relations will help us, we must take hold to-morrow and do it ourselves.'" The old birds were excited this time. They said, "We must leave our nest to-night When a man decides to to do a thing for himself, and to do it at once, you may be pretty sure that it will be done."

## CHAPTER XXIV.

### RELATIONS TO OTHERS.

THUS far we have considered chiefly what may be called the duties that one owes to one's self. Nearly all that has been said would be true if one lived independently of all others, and had to seek only a peaceful and happy life.

But we do not live thus independently. Every one of us is united with others. He is a member of a family. He belongs to the town, to the state, to the nation, to the whole world of persons. He is connected with the past and the future as well as the present.

It has been sometimes thought that society was formed by the free choice of men who had before been independent, living each for himself, but who gave up a part of their liberty for the sake of the protection and aid that come from living with others. We now know that from the earliest times men have lived in social relations with one another.

Indeed, man would be nothing if there were taken from him what he has received, and what he is always receiving, from the community in which he lives.

Did you ever lose yourself in the city or in the woods? If you ever did, you can understand how dependent we all are upon those with whom we live.

It is a very strange and painful feeling that one has when he is lost in a city; especially if one is without money. One who is thus lost sees only strange streets, strange buildings, and strange people. If he seeks food or shelter, he is looked at coldly. He has stepped out of his place in the world, and is helpless and homeless, till he has found his place again, or has made a new one for himself.

One is still more helpless who is lost in the woods. The trees may wave, the sun shine, the flowers bloom, the birds sing; all may be beautiful: but one who is lost has no part in it all. He has no food but the berries, no shelter but the trees, no friend to whom he may speak.

This illustration shows how little any one of us amounts to when he is left wholly to himself; and how we really live in the social life around us.

You have all read, I hope, the story of Robinson Crusoe. You may think that there was a man who lived by himself, and independent of the world.

But think, how sad he was, and how he longed to be with human beings once again.

Think, also, how much he took with him that other people had made, without which he would have perished. He had food with which to begin his life on the island; he had tools with which to provide for his needs. All these things and other conveniences were the product of the civilization that he had left.

Notice, further, that in making a place to live, in making a boat to sail in, and in whatever else he did, he was acting according to the experience that he had had, and the observation that he had made before he left home.

When he went beyond all that his experience had given him, he used the results of the training that he had had, and the habits of mind that he had inherited from the past.

He was thus simply a member of European society, a representative of European civilization, and a product of European history, who happened to be separated from the social world of which he was a part. He lived on the island, illustrating, as far as circumstances allowed, the results of European history and European civilization.

If he had belonged to a savage community, though he might in some things have done just what he really did do, yet he would, on the whole, have thought, felt, and acted like a savage instead of thinking, feeling, and acting as a European.

This illustration shows how impossible you would find it to live as if you were alone in the world. As I said before, if you could give up all that you have received from the past and from the social world of the present, there would be actually nothing left of you.

If a leaf on a tree could think, it would be just as easy for it to try to be something without regard to the other leaves and to the tree on which it grows, as for a man to try to be anything by and for himself, without regard to the social order of which he is a part and a product.

The leaf may fall from the tree and wither, but it is a leaf just the same : only it is a shrunken and withered leaf. So a man may try to live as if the rest of the world had no interest for him; but he cannot help being a part of this world: only, in trying to live without regard to it, he may lose something of the fullness and strength of his life, just as the fallen leaf loses so much of its beauty.

## CHAPTER XXV.

### SELFISHNESS.

IF thus no one lives merely for himself, but is a part of the community, the family, the town, the state, and the world to which he belongs, it is clear that one's first business in life is to fill his place properly and well.

One who would live merely for himself, without regard for others, is like a musician in a band or orchestra who seeks to make as much noise as he can, and thus attract attention to himself, instead of simply filling his place in the great whole. Such a one would attract attention to himself, but he would simply make himself disagreeable and ridiculous.

I do not mean that one is not to seek his own good or his own happiness. It would be a very dull and spiritless world if no one cared for his own interest or pleasure.

Indeed, if one does not take care of himself under ordinary circumstances, he cannot fill his place in the great body to which he belongs. The soldier must keep well and strong and in good spirits, or he cannot be what he should, in the march or the battle. Many a soldier who has been kept back by sickness or suffering from taking part in some difficult and perilous movement in which the army corps to which he belonged was taking part, has regretted his failure to be in his place and to do his share of the work, more than all the pain that he is suffering.

The world in which we live is like a great army, in which each has a place. The family, the school, all the relations in which one stands, are like the divisions of an army, at least in so far that each supplies a place in which one must stand, and gives also duties which belong to this place.

While, then, one seeks his own interest and pleasure, he is not to seek these as if other people did not have their own interests and pleasures, which are worth as much to them as his are to him.

The living as if one were alone in the world, or rather as if other people were in the world simply to serve us, is called selfishness. Selfishness consists in the disregard of others, and in seeking to fulfil one's own desires as if other people had neither desires nor rights.

Selfishness, we might almost say, is *the one bad thing* in the world, for all crimes and all misdeeds, great and small, spring from it.

It is selfishness that robs and cheats. The selfish man wants money. He does not care that others have also their wants and their rights. They have money and he wants it, so he takes it in any way that he can.

It is selfishness that is the source of intemperance and all the degradation and crime to which it leads. To see the drunkard, poor and ragged, despised and ridiculed, you would hardly think that he went into it for the sake of having a good time. If he went into it for that, it does not seem to have been a success.　But it is because at the first he thought merely of his own immediate pleasure, and forgot the happiness of father and mother, or of wife and children, that he sank to this low condition.

It is selfishness that leads to the neglect of the poor and the helpless, that makes men so stingy and mean that they are often unwilling to help others even when it can be done at little cost or trouble to themselves.

It is selfishness that speaks the cruel words or makes the jest that gives another pain.

It is selfishness that takes pleasure in tormenting another; that takes pleasure in tormenting the dumb animals.

In a word, selfishness seeks to get the most good possible out of the world, and to do the least that is possible for others.

It is easy from this to see what a mean thing it is to be selfish.　Indeed, what we call meanness is selfishness on a small scale.　But selfishness on a large scale is just as contemptible and just as mean as the other.　You have a contempt for the child that gets off by itself, so that it can eat its cake or candy without having to share it with its friends.　You have a greater contempt for the child that gets possession of its playmate's share of the good things that children love so much.　But selfishness of older people, in regard to things considered much more important and dignified, is just as mean and contemptible and childish as this　The selfishness of the great conqueror who gratifies his ambition at the cost of the lives or happiness of millions; or that of the demagogue who misleads the people, arousing their discontent and passion, that his schemes of ambition may be aided, is just as mean as that of the child that seizes its playmate's cake or apple.

## CHAPTER XXVI.

### OBEDIENCE.

WE have seen that every man is a member of the body that we call, in general, "Society." First he belongs to the family, and then through this to larger organizations. Selfishness we have found to be the attempt of a person to live as if he existed merely on his own account and as if other people existed for him.

There are several ways in which the relation to this common life makes itself felt. Some of these we will now consider.

One of the most outward, and yet one of the most important of these, is *obedience.*

It is obedience by which the man takes the place that belongs to him by yielding to the claims which society makes upon him.

These claims differ according to the age or the position of the person upon whom they are made. So far as one neglects them and lives merely on his own account, he loses, as we have seen, his best life.

The boy sometimes feels that it is childish to obey the rules of the home or the school. He feels that to set them at defiance is manly. On the contrary, *it is obedience that is manly and disobedience that is childish.*

The baby knows no rules. It seeks only what seems pleasant to itself. It is kept only by force from doing what would be harmful to itself, or to the persons and things about it.

Soon, however, in the case of a child properly trained, the rules begin, and it never is free of them again so long as it lives.

The first lesson that the child has to learn is the general one of obedience. *It must learn to obey*, for this lies behind and beneath all other lessons.

In the matter of obedience the training of a child is like the training of a dog or a horse. When the animal has learned what it is *to mind* it can learn a great many other things.

This does not mean that the child must have hard and harsh rules. The best obedience is learned quietly and pleasantly, and almost without the sense of constraint. Even a dog is best trained in this way, and then it thoroughly enjoys performing its tricks.

You may have been surprised at being told that it is manly to obey, and that men and women have to do this. At school the scholar has to mind the teacher, and the teacher seems only to command. But the teacher has to obey as truly as the scholar. What would you think if, when you went to school, you should find that the teacher had gone off for a day's pleasuring in the woods? You might like it, but what would your parents or the committee think? What would they think if the teacher did not hear your lessons, and did not see that you learned them? Thus you see that the teacher has to obey as well as the scholar.

What would you think of a shop-keeper who should shut up his shop every now and then, when he wanted a little fun? or of a doctor who, when he was sent for, should send back word that he was reading a novel and that he did not wish to leave off? In all such cases we should not say, "How manly these people are to do what they feel like doing, without regard to the demands that are made upon them." We should say, "How childish they are!" Thus you see that to obey is manly; to refuse to obey is childish.

The man has to obey more strict laws than the boy or the girl knows anything about. On a ship, the sailors think what an easy time the captain has. He seems to have nothing to do but to give orders. But the sailors, except when the weather is especially bad, have their hours of work and their hours of freedom; their watch above and their watch below. But the captain is never quite free. He not only has to obey the orders of the owners of the ship, but, in doing this, he has to have thought for everything, for the wind and the currents, for the barometer and the clouds. He is subject thus not merely to the direct orders of the ship's owners, but to every change of wind, and to all the facts about him, to what we may call *the law of things*.

This *law of things* is more pressing and continuous than any other. It is to this that men and women are especially subject.

Above all there is the law of duty, the obligation to do right, from which one can never escape.

Obedience is in life what subjection to law is in the natural world. It is obedience that keeps the planets in their places, and brings seed-time and harvest each in its season; just as it is obedience that makes all the difference between a civilized society and a horde of savages

This is what Wordsworth had in mind when in his magnificent "Ode to Duty" he exclaimed:

" Thou dost preserve the stars from wrong;
And the most ancient heavens, through Thee, are fresh and strong."

One who has not learned to obey can hardly find a pleasant or satisfactory position in a world that both physically and socially is held together by obedience.

## CHAPTER XXVII.

### LOVE AND SYMPATHY.

EVERY person, as we have seen, is bound to the social order by obligations that require obedience. This bond is, however, an outward one. *There is an inner bond* which is even more important, by which each one of us is, or should be, united to those about him. This is *love* or *sympathy*.

A little while ago we saw that no man can live by and for himself, and that we are dependent upon the world of men and women, the world of the present and the world of the past, for all that we have and are. The same thing may be more clearly seen in the fact that any person becomes unhappy if long separated from his kind. We all need the companionship, the sympathy, and the love of others. Hardly any punishment is so severe as a long term of solitary imprisonment. In Hawthorne's story, "The House of the Seven Gables," the character of Clifford Pyncheon shows how a person becomes weakened and stupefied by such imprisonment. It is indeed well for all sometimes to be alone. Too much and too constant intercourse with others may hinder our best life. But nothing is more painful and more dangerous to the best life than prolonged separation from other people.

I have known a case in which an ox, whose yoke-fellow had died, died itself shortly after from mere loneliness. Men and women are hardly less dependent upon companionship.

The world is so made that it probably never happens that a person lives who has not, or has never had, any one to love him. There is the love of parents, of brothers and sisters, of relatives and companions.

On the other hand, it is as rare to find a person who does not love some other person, or at least some animal; though some persons are so bound up in themselves that this love is very weak.

Love and sympathy may generally be regarded as stronger or weaker examples of the same thing, or as different aspects of the same thing. There may, however, be sympathy where there is no love, and love where there is little sympathy.

There may be sympathy without love, for you may sympathize with the grief of a person who is a stranger, and even with that of one whom you dislike.

It seems less natural that there can be love without sympathy. A person may, however, be selfish enough to cause pain to another whom he loves, with no thought of what he is doing. A young man may, by disobedience or evil habits, cause great grief to his parents whom he really loves.

Sympathy needs a certain thoughtfulness as its root. One must think of others and put himself in their place, and consider what will please and what will wound them. Strange as it may seem, nothing can be more cruel than love that is thoughtless in regard to its object.

Every one knows that other people have feelings like his own. But though we all know this, it takes some people a long while to really feel that it is so, to realize that others have feelings that can be pained.

Every one should have such a sense of this fact that he will shrink, by a kind of instinct, from giving another unnecessary pain, just as he shrinks from giving *himself* unnecessary pain.

We should thus extend our own personalities, so that we shall feel with and for others somewhat as if they were a part of ourselves.

This interest in others, whether it be love which we can feel only for a few, or sympathy which we should feel more or less for all, may take the hardness out of the duty and obedience which were spoken of in the last chapter

The doctor going to see his patient may go, not because it is his duty, or merely to gain this special fee, but because he is interested to help him. The boy may do what his parents wish because he loves to please them

If we cannot live without the companionship of others, and if we are all surrounded by affection and interest that give the charm to our lives, how careful should we be to meet such love and sympathy with a corresponding love, and a thoughtful sympathy, so that we shall not receive everything, and give nothing in return.

# CHAPTER XXVIII.

## USEFULNESS.

WE have seen that every one is, or should be, bound to the world of men and women, *outwardly by obedience, and inwardly by love and sympathy.* In these ways each becomes a member of the great organization that we call society.

Growing out of these is another form of relation as important as these, namely, that of *usefulness.*

Every one has a place in the world, and if he fills this place properly, he is of service to others and to the great body of which he is a member.

Notice the workmen when some large house is being built, and see how, while they are busied in many different ways, each one is helping on the common work. The hod-carrier carries up the bricks and mortar; the mason places the bricks carefully and evenly where they belong; the carpenter, the glazier, the painter, the slater, and all the rest, do some one kind of work, and others another; and all, under the direction of the contractor, carry out the plan of the architect, till what was at first merely a thought in the mind of the architect becomes a finished building, fitted for use, and perhaps' an object of beauty. From the architect to the hod-carrier, no one of the workmen could be spared.

We see the growth and the beauty of a tree. Here

also every part is of use.  The roots draw up the nour-
ishment from the soil.  The trunk and the limbs give
strength and form, and furnish channels through which
the sap runs to every part  The green leaves are the
lungs through which the tree breathes.  The flowers
and fruit prepare and cherish the seed from which other
trees spring.  The lightest leaf, the gayest flower, the
most thread-like rootlet that is hidden in the black
earth, all are of service, and each helps on the common
life.

Look now at the world of men and women, and see
how every calling is an opportunity for some form of
usefulness by which society is the gainer.  The doctor,
the lawyer, the minister, the shoemaker, the gardener,
the shopkeeper, the dressmaker, and all other workers,
are each filling a place in the great social body.  If
these places were not filled, the life of the world would
be lacking in something.

Men enter these callings for the most part, perhaps,
to get a living.  It is, however, an important fact that to
get a living, one needs, for the most part, to perform
some service; just as the flowers earn their right to
their place in the plant and to the sap that comes to
them, by preparing and protecting the germs that are
to become seeds.

The man that considers merely how much money he
can make by his labor, fills his place in the world very
poorly.  Think how grand and noble a thing all labor
would come to be, if each one would perform it with the
thought that by it he is doing his part for the well-being

of the world. Every one should make his life larger by the thought of the usefulness and the importance of what he is doing, and the thought that by it he is a living member of the great body.

We sometimes fancy that we would like to live merely to amuse ourselves, with no cares or duties. But when we think more carefully, we see that this would be a mean sort of life. One would be ashamed to have the whole world working for him, and he to be doing nothing for the world.

Besides these ways of usefulness that grow out of the various callings of life, one who has the love and the thoughtful sympathy that were spoken of in the last chapter, will find many other kinds of special helpfulness. There are always about us those for whom we can do something. People are always doing something for us in these little ways, and it would be mean not to do the like for them. Even if they were not helpful to us, that is no reason why we should not help them. We can pay to them a part of the debt that we owe to those who have helped us, but whom we have not helped.

For boys and girls in school or in college, the school or the college is their place of business. They are getting ready to take their part in the work of the world, just as the growing twig is getting ready to bear its part of the weight of leaves and fruit.

But while this preparation is going on, there are chances enough for helpfulness. These are found at home, among their companions, or with those whom they chance to meet; and everyone who has the right spirit will take both pleasure and pride in being helpful. One should be ashamed merely to be taken care of in the world without doing anybody any good, even if the interest that he has for others would let him.

As self-command is the fundamental principle of the ethics of Stoicism, and as the desire for happiness is that of the ethics of Epicureanism, so the principle of love and service is fundamental in the ethics of Jesus.

## CHAPTER XXIX.

### TRUTH AND HONESTY.

WE have seen that men are bound to society by obedience, love, and usefulness. There are certain virtues growing out of these principles, and certain vices corresponding to these, a few of which we will now consider.

Prominent among these virtues are those of *truth and honesty*. To these are opposed the vices of lying and cheating.

Society is like a building, which stands firm when its foundations are strong and all its timbers are sound. The man who cannot be trusted is to society what a bit of rotten timber is to a house.

How often we see the effects of dishonesty in the building of houses. Every now and then we read of some great crash, which has occurred because the contractor who was putting up a building had been dishonest. He had used poor material, or had put his material carelessly together. So the building falls perhaps even before it is finished.

Poor work is bad enough; but what the man *is*, is even worse and more harmful than what he *does*. He himself is a piece of rotten timber, to which no one can trust, and he is tending to make society itself as unstable as the house that he was pretending to build.

*Society exists because men trust one another.* On the

whole, men can be trusted, if one uses a reasonable care. The dishonest man thus does not belong to a civilized society  He belongs to the times of barbarism before men had learned the worth and importance of trust-worthiness.

He thus is in the position of a barbarian who is making war upon civilization, just as the hostile Indian lurks about some settlement in the wilderness, seeking to plunder and destroy.

What contempt we have for a man who robs another, who picks his pocket, or knocks him down in some lonely place and strips him of whatever articles of value he may have!  But the man who cheats, is a thief just as truly as the pickpocket and the robber.

There are kinds of cheating that the law cannot or does not touch.  The man who practises this kind of dishonesty is even worse than if he were doing that which the law punishes.  He uses the law which was meant to protect society as a cover from which he can attack society.

The boy who cheats in his games really spoils the games.  The game is not for the sake of the victory. It is the idea of the victory that gives zest to the game It is the playing according to rule, and the winning, if one can win according to the laws of the game, that give all the fun there is in it  Thus the boy that cheats does for the playground what the man that cheats does for society.

As the boy that cheats in his games puts himself outside the community of his playmates, and makes war upon it, so he, when he grows up to be a man, will probably be the one who will, by dishonesty, separate himself from society and make war upon it.

Lying is a form of dishonesty, and a very bad form of it. What would become of the world if we could not trust to one another's word?

A lie is told for one of two ends: either to get some advantage to which one has no real claim, in which case it is merely a form of cheating; or to defend one's self from the bad consequences of something that one has done, in which case it is cowardly.

It is always mean for a man or boy "to go back," as we say, on a friend. It is still worse, if possible, to "go back" on one's self. A brave man or boy will manfully take the consequences of his act, and if they are bad, will resolve to do better another time.

The worst sort of deceit is that by which one lets another bear the blame, or in any way suffer, for what one has one's self done. Such meanness happens sometimes, but it is almost too bad to be spoken of.

It is a great thing to call acts and actors by their right names. If we should always do this, I think it might save us from some faults.

If before speaking what is untrue, one should say to one's self, "That would be a lie, and if I should say it I should be a liar"; or if before doing a dishonest thing one should say to one's self, "If I should do this I should be a cheat," I think fewer false words would be spoken and fewer dishonest acts would be done.

## CHAPTER XXX.

### GOOD TEMPER.

A MAN with a bad temper, like one who lies and cheats, makes war upon his social surroundings : only he does in an open and bold way what the other does in a sly and underhand way; and, further, his war is with individuals, while one who lies and cheats attacks the very foundations of society.

It is not, however, always wrong to be angry. There are occasions when it would be wrong not to be angry. In these cases it is, indeed, war; but it is war in defence of society, not against it We do not call a man who is angry only when it is right to be angry, a man of bad temper.

If one sees a strong boy tormenting a small or weak one, or abusing some helpless animal, anger is a proper as well as a natural feeling. It is so, too, when one sees another imposing upon some one more ignorant or simple than himself, taking advantage of ignorance and simplicity.

One may sometimes be angry at wrongs done to one's self, when one has been treated brutally, or has been wickedly deceived.

Anger is in such cases a natural instinct of defence, by which one wards off or punishes injury to others, or to one's self.

In spite of this, anger, as it actually exists in the world, is more often wrong than right. It is for this reason that it is commonly spoken of as a fault.

It is a fault *when one gets angry too easily.* There are persons who lose their temper at any little thing. They are always thinking that others meant to injure them in something that they said or did. They are always thinking of their rights or their feelings.

Such anger is a form of selfishness. It comes in part from keeping the self prominent in one's thoughts, and thinking that whatever is said or done has had some reference to one's self.

This appears from the fact that such persons have very often less consideration for others than for themselves.

We should remember that anger is apt to be a very unjust judge. Nothing exaggerates like anger. To look at an act through an angry mood, is like looking at an object through a magnifying glass. It is often more like looking through a glass that distorts as well as magnifies. In anger, everything looks out of proportion.

One should be thoughtful to distinguish between what is meant and what is accidental. Even a dog will often show no anger if it thinks that one trod on it by accident; whereas if it thinks the hurt was intentional it will be filled with rage. We ought to be at least as considerate as a dog.

Because anger exaggerates, *the passion is often too strong* even where there may have been some real provocation.

" Anger," says an old Latin proverb, " is a short mad-ness." The boys say something of the same kind when they speak of being " mad," when they mean angry.

The person carried away with anger has no mastery of himself. He does not know what he is saying or what he is doing. He is really " beside himself." He sees nothing as it is Such a person is feeling very heroic, but he is often appearing very foolish and ridic-ulous.

*Anger is often unreasonable.* In anger we pronounce judgment upon another, perhaps upon our best friend. For the moment we see only his faults. We are com-plainant as well as judge. As the criminal has no ad-vocate, we should pause and plead his cause ourselves, and ask, " Is it certain that the accusation is true? Is the case quite as bad as it looks? Has this person, whom at other times we have loved, no good qualities? Is there nothing to be said in his defence? "

*Anger is often too long-lived*, even when it may have been at first justifiable. At the first moment of passion, perhaps, one can hardly pause to ask the questions that were just suggested; but after a little time one should be able to do this, and thus control the wrath.

If you are angry with a friend, you know, though you may not think it at the time, that the anger will not last forever. You may calm your rage by looking forward to the time when you shall be again at peace with your friend.

One should thus *learn to forgive* even when one has really been injured We should be able to see that the act that offended us was far less evil than it seemed at first; or that it does not represent the real or the whole person who offended us. Or at least we can judge it calmly, as if it had been done to another.

Some persons are by nature more quick-tempered than others. By giving way to the fault, we make it worse and worse; while by checking it, in such ways as have been named, we may gain the habit of keeping a better command over ourselves.

I need hardly speak of the advantages of having a good temper. Not only are one's relations to others the pleasanter for this, but one can even guard his own interests the better. The bad-tempered person is apt to harm himself more than he harms others.

## CHAPTER XXXI.

### COURTESY.

EARLY in this book, we saw that the words "morality" and "ethics" mean, in their etymology, simply manners; and we saw how this thought of manners formerly referred to the whole life. At present we use the word "manners," simply to express the most outward relations of life. We speak of "good manners" or "bad manners," meaning by the words that a person conforms more or less perfectly to what are called the "usages of good society." Thus a man may have good morals and bad manners, or he may have good manners and bad morals, or both his manners and his morals may be either good or bad.

Of course, if we have to choose between them, it is much better to have good morals than good manners A man's good manners may sometimes even help him to carry out wicked plans. In this case, we dislike him all the more for the good manners which he has used to help him in his wickedness.

But one does not have to choose between the two; and good manners, though less important than good morals, are yet very desirable.

Some kinds of bad manners do no harm to any one except to the person practising them. They are disagreeable to see, but their greatest effect is that the bad-mannered person shows himself to be a boor.

If a man keeps on his hat in another person's house, he simply shows himself unacquainted with what are regarded as the proprieties of life.

Now, it is not desirable to be a "dude" on the one side, or a boor on the other· but a little attention to these matters will help to make one agreeable to those whom one meets.

Young people sometimes think attention to such things is foolish. When I was a small boy, I thought it a ridiculous piece of affectation in the schoolmistress, who insisted that I should say "catch" instead of "ketch." Now I am grateful for the breaking up of any such bits of ill breeding.

Another kind of good manners is still more important. I refer to habits of courtesy towards all with whom we have anything to do.

Courtesy towards another *shows a certain respect for his personality.* We have seen that we should respect ourselves: it is hardly less important to show respect to others.

A habit of courtesy is like a delicate wrapping which prevents one personality from rubbing and chafing against another; and it thus prevents much of the friction and irritation of life.

Courtesy is perhaps most of all proper from the young towards those who are older than themselves. There is too little of this in our days. Boys and girls will speak to their elders, perhaps even to their parents, with rude familiarity, such as would be hardly proper among playmates.

When one meets even a stranger in any place where the two are brought together, a little greeting does much to take away the sense of strangeness  In Europe, when one enters a public conveyance, or seats himself at the table of a hotel, or meets another on a country road, there is almost always a pleasant greeting, such as is too rarely seen in this country.

The habit of courtesy from boys and men to ladies is another mark of good manners which is not to be neglected.

Ladies often show bad manners in taking such acts of courtesy as if they had a right to them  If a man offers a lady a seat, he has a little sense of injury if she seems to regard it as her due, and does not even thank him for what he has done.  This sort of ill manners in American women has tended to diminish such courtesy towards them.

One should show courtesy to his companions.  Boys, even in their play, should be courteous to one another. One who is always pushing for the best without regard to others shows his ill breeding.  A "thank you" and a "please" on proper occasions, are not out of place even among the closest companions.

Perhaps in the family, courtesy is more important than anywhere else; because hardly anywhere else are people thrown so closely together; and, thus, nowhere do they need more the protection of courtesy by which much unpleasant friction and much unhappiness would be avoided.

Courtesy is not something artificial.  It is simply an

expression of thoughtfulness for others, and rudeness and boorishness, though sometimes they spring from ignorance, are more often the expression of selfishness, which forgets the feelings and the tastes of others.

## CHAPTER XXXII.

### THE PLAYGROUND.

IT may seem strange to speak of duties in connection with play. One great charm of play is the escape from the sense of duty. At school one has to be very careful as to what he does and what he does not do. There are rules at every turn, but on the playground one escapes from rules.

There are rules of a sort, it is true. There are the rules of the game. There are also certain kinds of mischief that must not be done, and similar general regulations; but on the whole, on the playground one is free; and this makes a good part of the pleasure of the sport.

It is a very pleasant thing to feel one's self free; to be able to do just what one feels like doing. It is a freedom like that which I suppose a horse feels, when he is turned out to pasture, and can fling out his heels, or roll without any thought of whip or rein.

I do not wish to disturb the sense of freedom that you have at play. Indeed it is because the playground is so free a place that I speak of it here. *There is, perhaps, no time in the world when a person shows himself for just what he is, as truly as he does when he is amusing himself.* Then he has no rules to observe; he is off his guard, and whatever of good or bad there is in him is likely to show itself.

The playground is a little world by itself. On it may be displayed a great many of the virtues and the faults of the great world in which men and women live. I am sometimes tempted to think that a great deal that goes on in this larger world is little better than play of a very formal kind. But it is certain that the great world is reflected in the little world where boys and girls are at their games.

What an opportunity there is on the playground to show *the strength or the weakness of one's command over himself.* Some young people are always getting angry in their play. They make themselves very disagreeable to their companions. They may break up the merriest party or spoil the best time.

There are many opportunities to lose one's temper at play. It is not pleasant to lose the game; yet, from the nature of the case, some must lose it.

It is especially unpleasant to lose it by the bad play of some one on your own side, and it is very often the case that the game is lost in this way.

It is very easy to think that the other side has not played fairly, and to get angry over the suspicion or the belief.

It is very easy to get into a quarrel over the rules of the game.

In some games it is very easy to get hurt and to accuse some one of being the cause of it.

There are, indeed, more ways of losing one's temper than I have time or space to name. The boy or the girl who is quarrelsome, could not have a better field for showing this quality.

The boy or the girl of good temper and pleasant disposition has the same opportunity to show them. If one can meet all the chances of play pleasantly, he shows great self-command, and by this experience he is fitting himself more and more to take part in the great game of life. Even in the hardest tussle one should keep his temper. I was once passing a group of boys at play, and heard one of them exclaim, "Any boy that can't fight without getting mad, had better not fight at all." It was a wise saying, which has often since come to my mind.

*Selfishness* shows itself as easily on the playground as it does anywhere else.

How many there are who always want to have their own way. No matter what others prefer, everything must be just as these say. There are tyrants on the playground as truly as there ever were in Greece or Rome.

Sometimes these tyrants have their way because they are strong, and their playmates are afraid not to do as they wish. Sometimes, strange to say, they have their way because they are weak. They make such an ado when they do not have what they want that the others follow them for the sake of peace. They think they are leaders; they would be a little disgusted if they knew they were being treated like babies.

Selfishness may show itself in a hundred ways; in thoughtlessness of the feelings of others, in seeking what is pleasant to one's self without considering any one else, in taking more than one's share of what is pleasant.

All these things may be done under many different forms.

*Kindness and generosity* have their place in the play-ground. There may be a thoughtfulness for one who is weaker than the rest, or who is a new comer, or whom, for any reason, others may neglect. There is an opportunity to stand up for those who are ill-used. There is a generous sympathy for those who in any way are having a hard time.

There is an opportunity for *honesty and dishonesty* on the playground.[1] One may cheat in a game no less than in business, and can show honesty no less. Indeed, the term " fair play " is used in regard to the most serious affairs of life. In politics or in business of any kind, we hear it said, " Such a person did not have fair play." In this use of the word we see the standard of play applied to the actual affairs of life.

There is a great opportunity for *energy or laziness, presence of mind or carelessness,* to show itself on the playground.

In all these ways boys and girls, when they are at their play, *show pretty well what they are going to be in later life.* When Napoleon was at a military school, the boys were one day playing at war. One set of them held a fort which the others were trying to cap-ture. The boy, Napoleon, led the attacking party. In the midst of the fight there was a flourish of trumpets, and a party of officers entered who had come to inspect the school. The boys that held the fort forgot their

---

[1] See, also, chapter XXIX.

play, and stood staring at the entering group. Napoleon did not lose his head for a moment. He kept his party up to their work. He took advantage of the interruption, and when the besieged recovered their wits, their fort was captured. He was already the Napoleon who in the real battles of later years knew how to turn so many seemingly adverse circumstances to good account.

You may say, " I cannot think of all these things when I am playing; if I did, I should have no time to enjoy the game." This is very true. You can, however, think of them beforehand, and make up your mind what you will do and what you will not do, so firmly that your mind will obey when you are not thinking about it.[1]   Or if, in spite of your purpose, you do something that you meant not to do, you will remember it afterwards, and your displeasure with yourself will help you to do better another time.

---

[1] In the chapter on Conscience, I shall speak more fully of this power of self-command.

# CHAPTER XXXIII.

## FUN.

THE word " fun " as it is used by young people, includes a great deal. So far as I can understand, it means any kind of " a good time." Certainly a good play, such as was referred to in the last chapter, is called fun.

I shall here use the word fun in its stricter meaning. Fun, in this narrower sense, refers to " *what is funny.*" The word " funny " is itself used in a very loose way. In common speech whatever is surprising is sometimes called funny; sometimes even if it is something sad.

Properly speaking, only that is funny which is laughable. I wish then to speak in this chapter of what may be found comical by one or another, and of what is done or said for the sake of raising a laugh.

We may often find in kindly and innocent mirth both pleasure and refreshment. The opposite of mirth is seriousness. One who has no sense of fun takes everything seriously. It is not well for any one to be serious all the time. For one who is so the strain of life is often too hard.

President Lincoln was very fond of a funny story. He felt the strain and the burden of the war so strongly that, if it had not been for this relief, he would have broken down long before the war was over.

It is a great thing to be able to see the ludicrous side

of one's own mishaps or failures. What one person will grieve over, another will carry off with a laugh. One may make a mistake, for instance, or meet with an accident which is not very severe, and be mortified beyond measure. Another will see the funny side of it, and find only amusement. A person who can never see the funny side of such mishaps, goes through life as if he were riding in a carriage without springs. Every little inequality makes a bump.

In the same way one may see the ludicrous side of the troublesome blunders of others. I know a lady who had a very stupid gardener. She wondered why the bulbs that he had set out did not come up. At last she dug down to see what had happened. She found them all planted upside down. Of course she did not like it; but she amused herself with the absurdity of the thing, imagining them at some future day sprouting up in China to the wonder of the natives.

While fun is in itself a very good thing, it may, like almost anything else that is good, be made a very bad thing

It may be made a bad thing in two ways.

In the first place it is bad *when there is too much of it.*

While it is not well to take all things seriously, it is worse to take nothing seriously. The great business of life is serious, and one who finds only fun in everything keeps himself outside the reality of life. He is like a bit of thistledown which floats about in the wind, while it has no real connection with anything

In the second place fun may become a bad thing, *because it is not of the right kind.*

In the chapter on " Different Kinds of Heroes " we saw that a person may be judged pretty fairly by what he admires. The object of his admiration shows the kind of person he would like to be. A person may be judged about as truly by what he finds funny as by what he admires.

One kind of fun which is wrong is that which gives pain to others, or which makes sport of the misfortunes of others.

There is hardly anything so painful or unfortunate that some will not be found who will laugh at it. The savages were sometimes in the habit of tormenting their captives. The tortures that these underwent were to them an occasion of mirth  Boys sometimes torment insects or animals because their struggles seem to them funny.

If we were without the feeling of sympathy, almost any weakness or suffering might seem comical. Thus to some the infirmities of age, or any deformity in the person of another, seem fit objects of ridicule.

In all such cases a feeling of sympathy would change the mirth into pity, or a friendly and helpful interest.

It would do this in two ways. In the first place we should feel so sorry for the persons afflicted that we should not feel like laughing at them ; and in the second place, we should know that our ridicule, if they should be aware of it, would add to their pain.

A kind sympathy would therefore make it impossible

to laugh at the infirmities or misfortunes of others. Those who do this show themselves unfeeling and cruel. They put themselves on the level of the savages.

The same kindly feeling would forbid jests that would in any way give pain to others. The idea of wit which some people have is to say sharp things to another, perhaps to twit him with something of which it is supposed he would be ashamed.

A person of good feeling would never find sport in what gives another pain.

I have read a story of a youth, who, while walking out with his tutor, saw a pair of shoes that a poor laborer had left under a hedge while he was busied with his work "What fun it would be," exclaimed the young man, "to hide these shoes, and then to conceal ourselves behind the hedge, and see the man's surprise and excitement when he can not find them." "I will tell you what would be better sport," said the tutor, "put a piece of money into one of the shoes, and then hide and watch his surprise when he finds it." This the young man did, and the joy and wonder of the poor laborer when he found the money in his shoe was as good fun as he wanted.

It is much better sport to plan pleasant surprises for people than to prepare unpleasant ones.

While we should not make jests that will give another pain, we should, on the other hand, not be too sensitive at jokes that are played on us.

Some people are very much annoyed, or perhaps lose

their temper, if they are laughed at. It very often happens that those that are most ready to laugh at others are the most displeased when the laugh is against them.

Such sensitiveness is very weak; and a person who is so weak makes sometimes an unpleasant companion. We all laugh at one another sometimes in a friendly way, and one who is never willing to be the object of such kindly mirth may interrupt the pleasure of his companions.

You should try not to be a person in regard to whom your companions will always feel obliged to consider at every turn, whether your sensitive feelings are likely to be hurt. "*One must take as well as give*" is a good motto for the rough and tumble sport and business of the world; just as "*One must give as well as take*," is a good motto, so far as the pleasures of life are concerned.

Another kind of joke which is wrong is that which is filthy and indecent. It seems to some persons a great stroke of wit to say something which would offend natural modesty. There is no kind of wit which is so cheap, and no kind, of which anybody who would be in the true sense of the word a gentleman, should be so ashamed.

Another kind of joke which a right feeling would avoid, is that aimed at what is to others an object of reverence. To some, profanity seems witty as well as manly. This is also a very cheap kind of joke which needs no wit for its making. It also shows low and unmanly tastes.

We find, then, three kinds of jest which a right feeling person will avoid: the unkind, the indecent, and the profane.

The play of wit and humor is thus very much like other play. It is one of the pleasant and helpful things in life. Like other play, it must be kindly, good-tempered, and pure. Like other play, it must not make up the whole of life. Rightly used, it may be one of the best helps in bearing the burden and doing the work of the world.

## CHAPTER XXXIV.

### FRIENDSHIP.

WHILE we should be courteous towards all with whom we are brought into relation, and should take part in the life that is going on about us, we cannot be equally intimate with all. Thus within the larger circle of associates are formed smaller groups of those who are specially bound together as friends.

What are known as friendships may be the result of various causes.

Perhaps most often those who call one another friends are those *whom some chance has brought together*, and who are specially united in work or play. In this way friends are often simply those who amuse one another.

Sometimes one considers another his friend *because he is flattered by him*. This flattery may be either direct or indirect. It is direct when it is open praise. It is indirect when it is a conformity to one's moods, tastes, or prejudices. If one thinks that he has been ill-used, it is pleasant to have another join with him in indignation. It is pleasant to have all one's jealousies, ill-tempers, and vanities thus sympathized with. Tyrants can often find no other friendship than this; and boys and girls have sometimes such hangers on, who think it worth the while thus to flatter them. The boy or girl of right feeling will find nothing more disgusting than this sort of companionship.

True friendships are based upon two things.

One of these things is *liking*, and the other is *respect*.

People *like* one another when each finds the other pleasant company    They have such similarity in tastes and interests that they like to be together.

For real friendship, however, this is not enough. For this, *respect* must be added to liking  You may think it strange to speak of boys and girls respecting one another.    You may think that respect is to be felt towards older people only.    But boys and girls may be as worthy of respect as men and women

A woman got into a street car the other day somewhat burdened with bundles.    A little girl of some ten or twelve years at once sprang up and gave her a seat. The child took her place by the side of her father, who had just given up his seat in a similar way.    As she stood there, holding her father's hand, with a sweet look on her face, I could not help respecting her for her act of kindness, and for the pleasant way in which it was performed

. Boys and girls who are honest and brave, to whose honor and kindness you may trust, these are worthy of respect.    If you will think of your companions, you will find that some you respect, and some perhaps you do not.    Those whom you respect may be as full of fun as the others, but there is to them something besides fun

You want for a friend some one whom you would like to have with you in trouble, should you meet it, as well as in sport; such a one is one who has your respect.

Choose, then, for your friends, those whom you can respect, and always act so as yourself to deserve the respect of your friends and companions.

Nothing adds more to the pleasantness of life than friendships. *Friendships involve, however, certain duties;* and we have now to notice some of these.

If one has a friend, *one should be loyal to him.* This loyalty may show itself in several ways.

If one is with those who speak ill of his friend, it is very base to join in such evil speaking. It is very base, for instance, to join in ridiculing a friend, except in a way that he himself would regard as a harmless jest. One should stand up for one's friend when he is thus spoken ill of.

Loyalty to a friend is shown *in looking out for his interest* and helping his plans in every honorable way.

One should *not be jealous* of one's friend. Such jealousy may show itself in either of two ways.

One of these ways grows out of the desire to monopolize the interest of a friend. Some persons are troubled if their friend does not seem to be wholly bound up in them. They do not realize that the larger the life of their friend is, the better worth having is his friendship.

There is another kind of jealousy which it is more difficult to avoid. I mean the unpleasant feeling that may arise if one's friend gets, as we say, "*ahead*" of him. Friends are apt to be pretty nearly equal in many ways, so that a feeling of rivalry may very easily arise. This is so common that there is a familiar saying to the effect that a man always has a certain pleasure in hearing of the misfortunes of his best friends.  I have seen in "Punch" a picture of a man reading a magazine with a pleased look on his face.  His friend, entering, notices this, and asks, "Are you reading a favorable notice of your book?"  "No," is the answer; "I am reading an unfavorable notice of yours."  For the reason stated above, such things may easily happen among those who call themselves friends.

A true friend will rejoice in his friend's successes and sorrow in his defeats as though they were his own.  There is nothing more beautiful than such unselfish sympathy.

A true friend sometimes finds it harder to bear the trouble of his friend than his own misfortunes.  One can make light to himself of his own suffering and call himself weak for yielding to it; but it would seem harsh to treat in this way his friend's misfortune.

While you do well to seek from your friend sympathy in your own trouble, *do not overburden him with petty complaints and discontents.*

Show yourself brave and strong, and be sure that you will receive more sympathy from your friend than if you whine and grumble.  If he sees you trying to make light of your trouble, it will seem to him more real   If you make too much of it, he will tend to make light of it.

Be honest with your friend.  Express frankly your own thought.  No true person wishes a friend to be what Emerson calls a "mush of concessions."  If you do not show that you have a character and personality of your own, what is there for your friend to respect or love?

*If your friend does wrong*, tell him kindly and honestly  A friend who will not thus advise is not worth the having.

If your friend reminds you kindly of your faults, take what he says not only pleasantly, but thankfully.  Few treasures are worth as much as a friend who is wise and helpful.  Such a one alone can remind us of our faults

While you seek in all honorable ways to serve your friend, *never say for him what is false, or do for him what is dishonorable.*

I once heard a man say, as the highest praise of another business man, that he would not do a dishonorable thing to oblige a friend.

In school, no less than in business life, one is often tempted to say what is false, or to do what is dishonorable for the sake of a friend.  This a true friend will never ask.  If, when you refuse to do this, your friend thinks that you show your lack of regard, you can answer him in the spirit of words of the poet,[1]

> " I could not love thee, dear, so much
> Loved I not honor more."

---

[1] Lovelace, " To Jocasta, on going to the wars."

## CHAPTER XXXV.

### THE HOME.

BESIDES the friendships which we form in the world are those which grow up naturally in our homes and which are apt to be, as they ought to be, the closest and the dearest of any.

Almost all living creatures have their homes. The birds have their nests, the wild beasts their dens, the bees their hives.

To almost all creatures these homes are the dearest places in the world. How gladly the birds fly to their nests at night! How frightened are the parent birds if a stranger approaches the nest where their little ones are! How fierce are the wild beasts if any one draws near their lair! Nothing rouses the fear or the rage of these lower creatures so much as anything that seems to threaten the quiet of their homes. How eager a horse is to get back to the stable, often so very dismal, which is his home.

To men, also, the home is apt to be, and should be, the dearest place on earth. I suppose that no song was ever sung so often or by so many people in widely distant lands as that which is so familiar to us all, and which many can sing who can sing little else, — the song of which the refrain is,

" Home, home, sweet, sweet home."

Though the animals have homes as we do, their relation to their homes is very different from our relation to our homes.

Think how little while the animals are interested in their young, and how soon the young cease to care for their parents and for one another. The young come into the world, and live together for a little while. The parents take care of them. They feed them and keep them warm; they fight for them if need be; sometimes they will even die for them. But very soon the little group breaks up. The young birds, for instance, in a few weeks grow strong enough to fly. They leave their nests, and scatter, this way and that. In time they build nests of their own, and I do not know whether they would recognize one another or the parent birds again.

In our homes, boys and girls live for years before they are able to take care of themselves. When at last they go out into the world and have homes of their own, they still remember one another and love one another, and still remember with love and gratitude the parents to whom they owe so much.

To many the home in which their childhood was passed continues, as long as they live, to be among the places that they love the most; and it is a great joy if now and then, perhaps on Thanksgiving day or Christmas, they can go back to it again.

The fact that children are so long in growing up, and pass so many years together under the care of their father and mother, is most important in the history of the race. During this long period of growth in the home they become fitted, as they could not in any other way, to take their place in the larger world of men and women. If children remained in their home as short a time as the young of the animals do, it is probable that men would have never risen above the state of barbarians. The home has been the great civilizer of the world.

We have seen in other chapters the importance in the world of sympathy and affection, of obedience and trustfulness. All these are learned in the family as they could not so well be learned anywhere else.

Through the habit of *loving* brothers and sisters and parents men came very slowly to have somewhat the same regard for other persons. Through *obedience* to the commands of parents men have formed the *habit* of obedience, so that they submit easily to the laws of society. Thus it is very largely through the influence of the home, and from the fact that our childhood lasts so many years, that the race of man has risen from barbarism to civilization.

The life in the home, which is so important, and which is to most so pleasant, involves many duties, a few of which we will notice.

Since the home ought to be one of the *pleasantest* places in the world, it is the duty of every member of a family to try to make it so. Rude ways of acting and speaking, which would be faults anywhere, are greater faults at home than anywhere else.

I have spoken of home as if it were almost always

pleasant. It is not always so. To some their home is very dreary. The trouble is, often, that some, or perhaps all, do not try to make it pleasant. They live each for himself, and do not care how much they may wound those about them.

Some persons are pleasanter and more courteous anywhere else than they are at home. A voice that is very sweet when addressed to outside friends or acquaintances, becomes sometimes sharp and petulant when addressed to members of the family. Some who are very gracious and thoughtful towards other people, are very rude and inconsiderate towards those who belong to their own household.

Some persons, young and old, in their own family are interested only in their own affairs. At home they are silent and absorbed, though when they go out into the world they may be lively enough.

One should be more courteous, more polite, more thoughtful, more entertaining, and more helpful at home than anywhere else.

It is indeed only those who are courteous at home that are really courteous anywhere; for if they are rude there, their manners in the outside world do not really belong to them They are put on like their fine dress, and are taken off again with that.

Some people, too, are *slovenly* at home, who look very well when they go anywhere else. But home should be always neat as well as pleasant.

But you may say, " Is there no place, then, where one can be himself ? where one can be free and easy

without being troubled by the thought of how he ought
to speak and act and look?"

But what do you really consider yourself? or what
kind of a self do you want? When you are fretful, and
disobliging, and sulky, and bound up in your own plans
or amusements, are you most really yourself? Are you
not truly yourself when you are kind and thoughtful for
others, when by a pleasant word or kind act you make
those about you happier? This at any rate is what
ought to be yourself.

Such a life as I have described in the family has two
results. It makes the home pleasant, and it makes the
boy or the girl really pleasant.

When one who has lived like this at home goes out
into the world, he does not need to put on a show of
good manners. His good manners have become a part
of himself.

Thus the family may do for young people now what
it has been doing for the world all along; that is, it
may civilize them.

To civilize is obviously to make civil. The uncivil
person is an uncivilized person. That is, he is so far a
barbarian. The most natural place to learn to be civil
is the home; though one who has not learned it there,
must try to learn it where he can.

In the chapter on Obedience I have spoken of the
obedience due to parents. This is the first duty of a
child, except in the rare cases where the parent commands something that is really wrong

The son and the daughter should also try to help

their parents, and should do this, not as a matter of duty, but out of love and interest. The boy should not fret at having to bring wood, or to do something in the garden, or to run on an errand. The daughter should try to find little things that she can do about the house. She should be glad to do a little sewing, to help to care for the younger children, and especially to take care of her own things. Sons and daughters should do this out of interest, because it is their home. Few things will please the father and mother more than such interest in the home.

Sometimes the children have had advantages that their parents did not have. Whatever good they may have gained in this way they should try to use in such a way as to make the home pleasanter and happier.

There is very much that brothers and sisters can do for one another. This relationship ought to be one of the pleasantest and most helpful in life.

Girls are apt to be more gentle and refined than boys; they can thus do very much to make their brothers gentler; not so much by formal lecturing as by the influence that comes naturally from intercourse with them. Advice, when it is needed, from a sister to a brother, if it is kindly given, may often do very much good.

Darwin, who was one of the most famous students of nature, tells us that it was his sisters who made him humane; that is, who made him kind and thoughtful. He began his studies of nature when he was a boy. He made collections of birds' eggs. Through the influence of his sisters he became so thoughtful for the birds that he used to take only a single egg out of a nest, so that the old birds should not be troubled because their little home had been broken up.

Young men are apt to think that young women are in some respects better than they. A sister may at least do something to make her brother keep this respect for women, which may be an important thing in his life. She may do this simply by the force of her own character, not setting herself up as though she were above him, but simply by being true and kind and sympathetic.

Then, too, a sister should be glad to help her brother as he may need with her needle and other womanly implements. The boy is very helpless about many little things with which the girl is quite at home.

The brother can help the sister in his turn. He is stronger than she, and can do many a little service in return for what he has received. He should be glad to put his strength and courage and activity at her service.

If brothers can be so much to their sisters, and sisters to their brothers, none the less may sister be helpful to sister, and brother to brother.

It is a great thing to have so near a friend as a brother or a sister, to whom one may confide whatever happens to fill his heart, to whom one may always look for sympathy and aid.

I know that the relation of brothers and sisters is sometimes very different from this. It is a great pity, when the good and the pleasure that may come from this relationship are lost. When they are lost it is always through somebody's fault. Be very careful that it is not through yours.

# CHAPTER XXXVI.

## THE SCHOOL.

As was implied in the chapter on Obedience,[1] the school is the scholar's place of business. From this several things will follow.

One is, that you should be *regular* in attendance. You should always be at school, unless there is some really important reason why you cannot. What should you think of a clerk who should stay away from his place whenever he had a mind to?

The mere attendance at school *is training in regularity*. Unless one has a habit of regularity he will accomplish very little in the world. Irregularity in attendance also *breaks up the work of the school*. It interrupts the connection of one day's work with that of the next, besides burdening the scholar with extra work to make up for lost time.

Try always to be *in season*. What would you think of a clerk who should drop into the office or the store half an hour behind time? I am afraid one who should do this often would soon be told that he need not come any more.

There are few more important habits than that of *punctuality*, and in order to be sure of being punc-

---

[1] Chapter XXVI.

tual one should make it a habit.   There is, on the other hand, no habit more easily formed, or more troublesome, than that of always being a little behindhand in an appointment.

Suppose one who has to meet half a dozen persons at a given hour is ten minutes late.   He puts back the business ten minutes, and will have wasted just an hour of other people's time.

The scholar who is late at school *wastes other people's time* as well as his own.   What a disturbance it is when he comes lounging in and interrupts all the other scholars at their work.

Always come *neat and clean* to the school.   An employer would soon dismiss a clerk who should come with unwashed face and hands, and with untidy clothes. The scholar who comes to school untidy and unwashed disgraces his home as well as himself.   No matter if it is his own fault, it is the home that will bear much of the shame of it.   Who would want to disgrace his home?

Be *honest* at school.   Scholars sometimes borrow pencils, paper, and other things, and do not return or replace them.   Books and instruments that belong to the school are sometimes kept by the scholar.   False excuses for failures are sometimes given.   All these things are as bad as any other dishonesty.

At school *attend to the work of the school.*   What should you think of a clerk at his desk who, instead of keeping accounts, should draw pictures in his account books, or get up sly games with the other clerks.   I fancy that he would very soon be told that he might amuse himself elsewhere.

I have said that the school is your place of business. I must now add that it is the place of *your* business. It is for yourself that you are working at the school, and for nobody else. Your parents and friends are interested in your success, but it is because your success in school will fit you for success later in the world.

While the school is, as I have said, the place of *your* business, you may be helped to fulfil its duties, by remembering the disappointment which your failure would cause to your parents and friends.

You have perhaps heard of the famous French scientist, Pasteur, to whom so many people that have been bitten by mad dogs, have been sent from this country. The discovery that he made in regard to the cause and nature of hydrophobia is only one of many which have been of the greatest service to mankind. When he was a boy at school, Pasteur at first neglected his studies. He preferred fishing and other amusements to the work of the school. At last, however, he realized that his father, who had little means, was making great sacrifices in order that he might obtain an education. He then began to study in good earnest. It was the thought of what he owed to his father that made him what he is

The scholar sometimes thinks of the teacher as if he were his enemy. The teacher is called a " master," or " mistress," and the scholar feels himself to be in some sort a slave. Really the teacher is simply working for the scholar. He is his helper, performing for him one of the greatest services that can be done

College students used sometimes to carry away the chapel bell and hide it. They did this partly for the fun of the thing, and partly, perhaps, with the idea that the absence of the bell would be an excuse for irregularity in attendance on college exercises. In most cases a great disturbance was made about such an act. There was a great examination of students, a great search for the bell, and threats of punishment for the offender. In one case, however, the president of the college simply said to the students, "Young gentlemen, the bell was solely for your convenience. It was thought that it would help you to wake in the morning, and to be regular in attendance at college exercises. If you do not want it, it is none of our affair. We shall take no trouble to find it. You may do without it as long as you like. But no student will be excused from absence or tardiness on account of the absence of the bell." I need hardly say that the bell was soon in its place.

All the rules of the school are like the chapel bell, simply helps to the scholar in doing the work of the school. Like the chapel bell they are on his account; only he cannot be left to choose whether he will, or will not, disregard them; for by such disregard his life may be greatly harmed.

I know that young people are restless and fond of sport. I know that the sunlight out of doors looks very pleasant, and the thought of play is very attractive, and I know that their attention is very easily turned; in a word, that they are bubbling over with life and activity. This makes it all the harder for them to do the work which is needed, in order that they may be fitted to take their place later in the world. These facts show the importance of the rules that seem so hard. They are *helps* in doing what the scholar cannot afford to leave undone, and which most young people could hardly do without.

Think how many have toiled under the most painful circumstances to get knowledge.

William Cobbett, who was a distinguished writer on political subjects in England, was in his youth a private soldier, receiving as wages only six pence (about twelve and a half cents) a day. He tells us how he studied. When he needed a book, a pen, or paper, he had to go without some portion of food, though he was half-starved. The edge of his berth when at sea, or that of his guard-bed when on shore, was his seat to study in In the winter he could have no light, except that of the fire, and that only in his turn. In this way he pursued the studies that are made so easy for you at school, especially English Grammar, which interested him greatly.[1]

When Lincoln was practising law, he interrupted his business in order to study mathematics, so as to learn what it is " to demonstrate."

Charles James Fox was a distinguished English statesman. When he was appointed Secretary of State, he took writing-lessons like a schoolboy, because some one criticised his handwriting.

---

[1] See Smiles' " Self Help," which contains many incidents of similar earnestness.

These men, as many others have done, pursued under great hardship, or at great personal inconvenience, studies that are made easy to those that **can** go to school. At school the scholar has books, time, help, and every thing that is needed for his work.   Yet some think it is hard to do, even under these pleasant circumstances, what others have thought worth doing under great difficulty. Yet what they learned was of no more value to them than the learning that is forced into the laziest schoolboy is to him ; except that by their energy they could make better use of it.

# CHAPTER XXXVII.

## PATRIOTISM.

As it is natural to love our home, it is also natural to love our country. As the poorest homes are sometimes most tenderly loved, so the poorest and barest country is sometimes held in most affection. There was perhaps never a country in the world the inhabitants of which have not, at some time or other, been willing to suffer and die for it.

Such affection is natural, because the town and the nation in which one has lived is, like the home, bound up with all the experiences of one's life. The games of childhood, the affection of parents, the love of friends, all the joys, the sorrows, the activities of life, are bound up in the thought of one's native land; so that men have felt for their country an affection made up of all their other affections.

The love of one's country is called Patriotism.

It is not merely natural to be patriotic; it is reasonable and right. Nearly all that makes life pleasant and desirable comes through the town or the nation to which we belong. Thus our gratitude should make them dear to us.

Think how many thousands in our country have toiled for us! They have made roads and they have built churches and schoolhouses. They have established mails and post-offices. They have cultivated farms to provide for our needs, and have built ships that cross the ocean to bring to us the good things which we could not produce at home. They have provided protection against wrong-doers. So, if we sleep in peace, and work and study and play in safety, and are wise and trained in the various arts of life, it is to the town and the nation that we owe nearly all these advantages.

Then too, in every nation such good results have been produced at great cost of suffering and life. *It is because there have been patriots who have loved their country better than they loved themselves*, that we have a country that we can love.

The American especially ought to love his country, because, in it, some of these results are reached more perfectly than elsewhere. There is no country in which the people are so free, and in which the freedom of one interferes so little with the freedom of all the rest.

We are so accustomed to see men of every class and condition going to the polls, and voting for what are called their rulers, though more truly they should be called the servants of the people, that it seems to us a wholly natural and common thing. We often forget that this is something very uncommon; and that there are those in other countries who look with longing at the freedom which we enjoy.

Such liberty is extending more and more in the world, but it is largely through the example of our country that this extension of liberty is accomplished.

Our liberty and the other blessings that go with it have

been bought at a great price. No nation has had more splendid heroes, who have braved all danger for their country, who have toiled for it, and suffered and died for it than America

When the bells are ringing and the cannon are firing on the Fourth of July, you must not think merely of the noise and the fun. You must remember those who on that day agreed that they would risk their lives and everything that was dear to them, that their country might be free. You must think not merely of those, but of those also who at other times of peril have given themselves for their nation's good, of those who found the land a wilderness, and suffered pain and privation, while they made the beginning of a nation. You must think also of those who ever since that time, whenever the liberty or the unity of the nation was in peril, have sprung to its defence.

These heroes are more in number than we can begin to name. There was one, however, whose name is so familiar that it has become commonplace to us, but who was one of the greatest heroes, and one of the best men, that ever lived. I mean George Washington. Through the whole world, his name stands for honor and courage, wisdom and patriotism. You must not let the fact that his name is so common make you forget that there are few heroes of history that deserve honor so truly as he.

At the end of the war of the revolution, Washington was at the head of a mighty army, and the object of the enthusiastic love of the whole people. He might easily have made of himself a king or an emperor. It was a marvel to the civilized world when he quietly laid down all this power. He twice suffered himself to be chosen President; and then he became simply a private citizen. This seems to us now the most natural thing in the world, but really it was something very rare; and gave him a fame such as few heroes of the world enjoy.

You cannot realize, as those of us do who remember it, the heroism that was shown in the war which preserved the union of our states, and put an end to slavery in our country. Young men gave up what was dearest to them in life; mothers sent their sons to the war, hardly hoping to see them again. These sacrifices were made for the sake of the country which they loved. You must remember this on " Memorial Day," and not merely look upon the day as a holiday, with a show of processions with flowers and music.

There have been heroes in peace as well as in war; men who have conquered the wilderness, who have upheld justice, and have helped on whatever was good and noble.

We ought, then, all to be patriots, and love the country which has done so much for us and at the cost of so many true lives.

But patriotism is not merely the loving of one's country, and the being proud of it. It has its duties as well as its pleasures. We should not be contented merely to take the good that others have won for us, doing nothing ourselves for the country for which they did so much.

There are those who are unworthy to live in our country because they are not willing to suffer the least inconvenience on its account.

There are those who are among the most prosperous in the land, who have received more good from the country than most others, who will not even take the trouble to go to the polls and vote. They will see their city misruled, and will not even take the trouble to cast the ballot that would help to save it.

There are many men who sell their votes. Think of all the cost of money and of noble lives at which our liberty has been won. Think how in many parts of the world men are looking with longing at the liberty which we enjoy; yet there are those to whom this hard-won freedom means an opportunity to make a little money by selling their vote.

There are those still worse. I mean those who find in politics an opportunity to make larger gains in meaner ways. They buy votes and sell those that they have bought. They make bargains and " deals." The welfare of the country does not concern them. They seek only their own gain.

There are those to whom the light laws that are over us seem grievous. They rebel against all restraint.

There are those who stir up excitement among the people, setting class against class, that they themselves may be advanced.

These things I name, that those who read these chapters may resolve that when they are old enough to have the rights of citizens, they will use them as patriots, and refrain from, and oppose, such corruption as I have described.

There are other ways of serving the country besides those that I have named.

All the private virtues, honesty and industry, are its best helps. Whatever tends to make men wiser and better is a service to the country.

The time may come, though I hope it will not, when it will be necessary to repeat the sacrifices of the past; to give money and life and what is dearer than life, that the nation may be preserved. If that time shall come, meet it as heroes met it in the past.

The country will one day be in the hands of those who are now boys and girls. Serve it and guard it, and do all that you can to promote its good.

# CHAPTER XXXVIII.

## KINDNESS TO ANIMALS.

WE have considered the importance of kindness and sympathy towards the persons with whom we have to do. We should show a like sympathy and kindness towards the dumb animals, which have, also, their place in our lives.

We all know that the animals can suffer as truly as men can, but there are many who do not realize this. If they did realize it, I think there would be less cruelty to them.

A young man once told me that, when he was a boy, he liked to torment living creatures, simply for the fun of the thing; but when some one explained to him that they really suffered, and that the movements which amused him were expressions of pain, he had a horror of such cruelty and never practised it again.

There are many reasons why we should be kind to animals. One is *because they are so much in our power.* The very fact of their weakness and our strength should make us merciful to them. To take advantage of our power is mean. It is like tormenting a child because it cannot help itself.

Another reason why we should be kind to animals is that *so often we have to take their lives. They are wholly at our mercy.* Some we have to use for food.

Others are injurious or unclean, and we have, in self-defence, to destroy them. This fact should give us a certain tenderness, so that we should avoid giving them useless pain.

So far as the domestic animals are concerned, *we owe so much to them that gratitude should make us kind.*

Here is a man, for instance, whose horse performs the work by which he earns money to live. One would think that gratitude, if not self-interest, would make him kind. How often the horse is half-fed. Perhaps the poor owner cannot always help this. But he can help beating him, and overloading him, and making him travel when he is so lame that he cannot step without suffering.

Those who do not mean to be unkind are often *cruel by thoughtlessness.* They leave the horse uncovered in the cold. They use too short a check-rein. They use a check-rein on a long journey, or with a heavy load, or when going up hill. In none of these cases should any check-rein be used.

Think how a dog loves its master, often in spite of cruelty; and yet how often is the master cruel!

The chief reason for kindness to animals is, however, that which I named first: *the fact that they really suffer.* What sort of man or boy can that be who can think it fun to cause suffering? One who can cause this should himself be made to suffer.

One good way to gain sympathy for animals is to *study about them and to observe them.* One who does this can hardly fail to get interested in them. He will find so much intelligence, so many curious ways of living, so much devotion and kindliness, that he will sympathize with them in spite, of himself. Even the fiercest beasts, for instance, have a devotion for their young, and will sometimes die in their defence.

One should not only be kind to animals one's self; one should so far as possible *prevent cruelty towards them.* If boys are persecuting some unhappy creature, if a man is unmerciful to his horse, it is a noble thing to interfere, if one can, in behalf of the oppressed. Many a boy or girl has thus done something to check the cruelty that is shown to some dumb beast, and thus to lessen, by so much, the suffering of the world.

# CHAPTER XXXIX.

### COMPANIONS.

WE have considered certain things which it is well to do, and others which it is well not to do.  We have now in a few chapters to consider certain helps and hindrances to right doing.

Nothing is more important in this respect than the kind of companions that one has  If a young man " goes," as we say, " to the bad," it is almost always on account of the kind of companions that he has had. On the other hand, companions may be as helpful as they may be misleading.

The reason for this influence of others is that *man is an imitative being;* that is, he tends to do what he sees people around him doing.

This imitativeness has been one of the greatest helps in the development of the world.  If a young child learned only what it was directly taught, it would learn comparatively little  Its chief education consists in seeing what those about it do, and in trying to do the same; and this kind of education goes on, more or less, as long as we live.

So the lower and more barbarous peoples have been raised by imitating the manner of life of more civilized peoples.

When we think of it, we see that *this tendency to imi-*

*tate is extremely natural.* I will state two or three things that will illustrate this.

A man has a tendency to perform any action or to speak any word of which he thinks. If a boy really thinks of striking another, he has a certain tendency to strike him. The reason he does not always do it is, that he thinks of other things at the same time. He thinks of possible punishment from parent or teacher; or he thinks that the boy will possibly strike back; or some regard for the boy may come into his mind; or he may think that it would be a low and mean thing to do.

If he does strike the other boy, it is because all these other thoughts for the moment disappear, and the thought of the blow, and of the offence which caused this thought, alone remain.

Now, in any occasion that may arise where we have to speak or act, *something that we have heard others say or do* under similar circumstances naturally comes into the mind, and with it comes a tendency to say or do the same.

Suppose, for instance, a boy has for his companions those who, when they are angry or anything goes wrong with them, use profane speech. When he is angry, or when anything goes wrong with him, the expressions that they use are the first that come to his thought, and with them comes a tendency to use the same. When he first went with them, he was perhaps offended or shocked by this kind of speech; but familiarity has taken away much or all of that feeling, so that, when these words come to his thought, the feeling which would keep them back has been very much lessened, if it has not been wholly destroyed.

What is true of profanity is true of any other kind of speech or act. It is difficult for a young person who lives much among those whose speech is faulty to continue to talk grammatically. This example shows how we tend to imitate our companions.

Much is said in these days about "hypnotism." We understand by hypnotism the fact that one person may be brought so under the influence of another, as to say and do, and even to see and think, only what the other suggests. If, for instance, the other suggests that there is a cow in the room, the hypnotized person will see a cow in the room, and will perhaps make great efforts to drive it away. It is doubtful if some grave crimes have not been committed in this manner.

In all this we see an exaggerated form of the kind of influence of which we have been speaking. The suggestion has such power, in this case, because it alone occupies the mind. The suggestions made by our ordinary companions, simply perhaps by their way of speaking and acting, tend to have a like influence. They control us less, because other influences are working in other directions; but almost every young person who falls into bad habits shows that these suggestions may sometimes get as complete control of a person as is the case in hypnotism.

Besides what are called "bad habits," there are other habits hardly less bad, that are caught from one's companions. Such are habits of frivolity, of unkind gossip, and whatever may tend to lower the standard of our lives.

Good habits of life, of thought, and of feeling are helped as truly by good companionship as they are hindered by bad.

If the nature of the companions among whom we live has such an incalculable influence over us, we see what power we have to shape our lives by the right choice of our companions.

We should remember, too, that we may as truly have influence over our companions as they over us. We should dread, more than almost anything else, the thought that another has been made worse by associating with us. To injure the nature of another is to do about as much harm as it is possible for us to do in this world.

## CHAPTER XL.

### READING.

THERE is a companionship that may be more helpful than any other; that is, the companionship of books. It is not always easy to meet the persons that we should most gladly choose as companions. In these days, however, it is possible for almost every one to obtain good books.

As books may be the most helpful of companions, so they may be the most harmful. As some books are better than our ordinary associates, so other books are worse than our companions, and have a power to corrupt that is all the greater because the books may follow us into our most lonely and quiet hours.

*Do not be afraid to read books that require a little thought.* How the muscles of the body grow soft and flabby when no strain is put upon them! So the mental fibres become relaxed and weak, when no strain is put upon them.

The mind is weakened also, rather than strengthened, by *reading too many books.* One goes to the library to get a book that he has never read. If it is a book that is just published, he is all the more pleased. He hurries through it, and then goes to the library again to get another book that is new to him.

In this way he gets very little good out of any of the

books he reads. What he reads passes through the mind so rapidly, and is so soon replaced by something else, that it makes very little definite impression The mind gets so used to looking out for something fresh, that it loses the interest, and thus the power, to grasp any thought or any information so as to hold it fast and make it its own.

We should laugh at a little girl who should say that she knew how to sew, when all she did was to draw the thread through the cloth, so that nothing remained of all that she was doing. Should we say that anyone who forgets as fast as he reads, knows how to read, any better than that little girl knew how to sew?

There is a proverb that says, "Beware of the man of one book." It means that a man who has taken a good book and read it, and re-read it, so as to get the mastery of it, will have vastly more power than another, who skims over one book eager to get hold of the next. Plutarch's Lives, for instance, thus studied, has formed a great many heroes.

Reading *affects the moral nature* and one's habit of feeling, for good or for evil, as much as it does the mind.

Many a boy has been utterly ruined by reading low novels; and many who have not been absolutely ruined have received a taint which has corrupted to some extent their lives.

On the other hand, many a man dates the beginning of his really manly life from the reading of some book that stimulated his best nature.

*The improvement or the lowering of one's taste* is of less importance, but still of real importance. It is a great thing in the world to be able to enjoy the best. Would it not be a pity to go to a picture gallery that contains some of the noblest pictures in the world, and find one's self unable to enjoy any except those that were low, or coarse, or worthless? So, in a world that contains so many noble books, it is very hard if one has trained his taste in such a way as to be able to enjoy only the poorest

It is this corruption of the taste which is one of the ways in which the reading of poor books harms the most. One thinks that he will, for a while, read wretched novels, and after that he will take something better. He finds, however, often that it is too late. He has spoiled his taste for what is good.

There are so many public libraries in these days, and books are so cheap, that every one of us has the best books at his command, as well as the worst. It is pleasant to think how many are making their lives better and stronger and nobler by such means. It is sad to think how many are ruining their minds and corrupting their hearts out of this abundance.

Try then to get hold of books that are worth reading. If you read a novel, take one that is strong and pure. One might as well go to the dram-shop or the opium den, as to devote himself to reading a kind of novel that is only too common.

Then there are the works on popular science that will tell you about this wonderful world; and there are the stories of great men that will show you how to make your life noble; there is the history of the past which, if it is well told, is, to an unspoiled mind, more interesting than many a novel. In a word, there is no limit to the healthful and helpful books that are at your command. In the midst of these, what a pity it would be if you should take only those that would do you harm.

## CHAPTER XLI.

### THE IMAGINATION.

THE mind is always busy.

You see a boy sitting on the door-step or lying under a tree. You say, perhaps, that he is doing nothing. He is doing something. In one way, he is pretty busy. He is *thinking*.

I do not mean that he is thinking seriously about something that interests him. I mean simply that there is passing through his mind a stream of thoughts more or less clear, and of fancies more or less distinct.

Perhaps, he is lazily recalling what he did yesterday, or planning what he will do to-morrow. Perhaps, he is idly watching something that is going on about him. Perhaps, if you should interrupt him, and ask what he was thinking about, he might really not know what to say, because all had been so vague. His wits, as we say, had been " wool gathering." But his mind had been busy, even if he has forgotten what it was busy about.

So if people are working, the man with his saw or hoe, the woman with her broom or her needle, their thoughts are busy all the time. Sometimes they are thinking about their work, sometimes about something very different; but their minds are never perfectly at rest.

It is strange to think of all these minds in the world always active, of our own minds always active, at least when we are awake; possibly when we are asleep.

Surely it is very important for us to consider what these busy minds are busied about, for nothing can affect our lives so much as this constant activity of our thought.

A person sometimes " talks to himself." It is a foolish habit, for he sometimes lets out secrets, and is overheard saying unpleasant things about the people who are present. But all this thinking that never stops is really a conversation with ourselves.

There is, then, a companionship with ourselves that is closer and more important than that with persons or books.

How important it is that the self with which we converse so constantly should be wise, pure, and well meaning

If any bad company does harm, the self, when it is not thus wise and pure and well-meaning, does more harm than any other companion.

In all this intercourse with ourselves, nothing is more important than what comes to us through the imagination.

As was implied above, there is a succession of pictures passing through the mind with other thoughts ; perhaps there are more pictures than any other kind of thoughts. These pictures are, for the most part, drawn very partially and imperfectly ; but they are distinct enough to let us know what they stand for, and to interest our minds.

These pictures are of what we have seen, of what we have read, of what we have fancied, of what we hope to see or to do, and of what we would like to do, when there is perhaps no hope of our doing it.

There is one very singular thing about these pictures. The more interested we are in them, or the oftener we turn to them, the more distinct do they become. It is as if, in a picture gallery, the paintings that the owner loved and that he visited every day should stand out bright and clear; while those for which he cared little should fade away.

In going through such a gallery we should learn exactly what the tastes of the owner are. So if we could just glance into one of these mental picture galleries, we could tell, better than in almost any other way, what sort of a person it is whose mind we are looking into.

We could tell not only what the person is: we could tell something of what he is going to be; for in this picture gallery the future is often represented before it becomes a fact. Indeed it is the picture that tends to give its shape to the life.

Temptation gains more power through these pictures of the imagination than in almost any other way.

A man sometimes does wrong by a sudden impulse, as when he strikes another in a moment of unreasoning rage; but for the most part the imagination prepares the way with its picturing.

A young man, for instance, is tempted to take money that does not belong to him. At first it is not a temptation; it is merely a fancy. He thinks what a nice thing it would be to have the money, and pictures the life he would lead with it. After this sort of imagery has pleased him for a while till it has grown so distinct as to haunt him, comes the vision of taking the money, the representation of one way or another in which it might be done without discovery, until these pictures also haunt him. We have already seen, in a former chapter, the way that suggestions affect the life. These suggestions of the imagination gain more and more power, until at last they fill the mind, and the man is almost forced to perform the act which he has gone over so often in his imagination. Through this repetition the deed has lost its repulsiveness, and has come to seem quite a matter of course.

What is true of this crime is true of other crimes and faults. The mind plays with the picture of them, until suddenly the picture has become a fact.

When evil imaginations do not become embodied in outward act, they yet of necessity corrupt and degrade the mind. Discontent, envy, anger, impurity, all nourish themselves by these pictures of the imagination, until the mind has become controlled and debased by them.

If evil imaginations have such power, when the imagination works purely and nobly it may become equally a power of good. The picturing of kindly and magnanimous acts may shape the life to their likeness.

A healthy imagination is also a source of true pleasure. By reading carefully, by keeping one's eyes open in the world, one may store the mind with pictures that will later bring satisfaction.

We should train the imagination to reproduce what we see. Most of us, when we see a beautiful landscape or picture, go away with the vaguest possible remembrance of it. It is a great help to re-picturing in the imagination, to be able to draw or paint. One who can do this has learned both to see and to re-produce. It is a good plan to look at an object, and then try to draw it from memory. If we çannot do this, it is well to close the eyes and try to recall a beautiful object that we have seen, and then to look at it again, and observe how far our mental picture corresponds with the fact. In this way we can train the imagination to remember, and make fine additions to our mental picture gallery.

In educating children, it is very important that we should give them opportunities to enrich their minds with pictures of something fair and pleasant.

There remains to be spoken of, a possible evil that may spring unawares from the imagination. The life may be harmed by living too much in the world of the imagination. The dreaming, even of good acts, may take the place of the performing of them, while the habit of revery, if unrestrained, too often assumes a form that is harmful to the strength and purity of the life.

## CHAPTER XLII.

### INDUSTRY.

INDUSTRY might well be urged as a duty. I wish, however, now to speak of it chiefly as an aid in accomplishing other duties. Few things are more helpful towards right living than industry, and few more conducive to wrong living than idleness.

When we speak of idleness, we must remember that no one is perfectly idle, excepting when asleep, and possibly not even then. We are always busy about something or other. If the hands and the feet are idle, the mind is always active. If it is not busy with study, or with some other useful occupation, it is busy with dreams and fancies. Even the Neapolitan beggars, lying stretched in the sun or the shadow, are talking or thinking or dreaming about something.

By industry we mean activity that is regular, and devoted to the carrying out of some purpose. More definitely, it is activity that is designed to be useful to ourselves or to others. It is thus a *regulated activity* by which our own welfare, or that of others, may be furthered.

We are apt to think, or at least to feel, that the necessity of working regularly is a hardship. Because as we get tired with our work we look forward with eagerness to the time of rest, we are apt to think that the pleasantest life would be one in which it should be all rest.

A little thought, however, will show us that the necessity of regular occupation which is laid upon most of us, is one of the great blessings of our lives.

Regular industry is helpful to the habit of self-command, which, as we have already seen, is of fundamental importance in our lives. Industry is helpful towards this in various ways.

In the first place industry is helpful to self-command because *the life is made regular by it.* Body and mind are by this regularity disciplined into a certain degree of orderliness. It is as much easier controlling body and mind when they are in such training, as it is for an officer to control a body of trained troops instead of an undisciplined mob.

Again a certain amount of activity *is more easily controlled* than inertia. You know that a ship must be going one or two knots an hour or she will not mind her helm. She must be making this way in her own course moved by the wind or steam or some other motive force. A ship that is merely drifting cannot be steered. Now in idleness we are simply drifting. The mind is lazily busy, but it moves according to any whim or impulse. Thus self-control becomes difficult if not impossible.

In idleness one is thus left to be more easily *the prey of any temptation.* When we are busy about something that interests us, this interest tends to keep out of the mind tempting thoughts; or if they enter, the mind, through this interest, being like a ship under good headway, keeps its course undisturbed by them. In idleness, however, the mind is more at the mercy of whatever

may occur. Thus idleness is the great foe to upright-
ness, purity, and earnestness of life.

It may seem more strange to be told that *industry is
one of the best helps towards contentment.* In fact, however, it is the idle who are apt to be not only the most
vicious, but the most unhappy. There being no regular vent for the activity of the life, the energies themselves tend to wear upon the life itself. The mind, not
regularly occupied, is open to all sorts of discontents and
envyings. Thus it dreams of what might be and compares it with what is, and makes itself wretched.

Indeed, activity is one of the greatest sources of happiness. In industry part of our energies, at least, are
regularly employed. However sweet rest may be in its
place, idleness soon becomes a burden.

The man indeed is happy who, when he has leisure,
knows how to give himself regular occupation. Most
of us however *do not know how to employ ourselves,* and
it is well that we should *be* employed.

It requires more genius to use leisure than to use
wealth. It is very important that the young should
provide interests for themselves, in studies or in philan-
thropic activity, so that, if later in life they have leisure,
it may not lie too heavily on their hands.

*Industry is essential for that usefulness* by which each
man may fill his place in the world. The lazy, like the
wicked, *may be made* useful. The Spartans used to send
a drunken slave through the city that the sight of his
folly and degradation might disgust young men with intemperance. He was made useful; he did not make

himself useful.   Every one should try to *make himself* useful.

From all this it will be seen that the necessity of labor is something at which we should rather rejoice than complain, and that habits of industry are the great helpers to virtue, happiness, and usefulness.

# CHAPTER XLIII.

## HABIT.

IN speaking of the influence of companions, I said that a man tends to imitate the persons by whom he is surrounded; and we saw that while this tendency may work harm, it may also work much good: and that, in fact, the development of civilization has been largely dependent upon this tendency.

Most of all, *a man tends to imitate himself.* The fact that he has done a thing once, in a certain way, makes it easier for him to do it again in the same way. The oftener this is repeated, the more fixed does the habit become. At last he cannot do the thing in a different way without great effort. Finally it may become almost impossible for him to do it in a different way.

It is interesting to see the force of habit in little things. Through these one can most easily get an idea of its real power.

Notice its power in such a little matter as putting on one's clothes, one's coat, for instance. Almost every one in doing this always puts the same arm first into the sleeve. With some it is the right arm and with some it is the left. Probably very few, if they were asked, could tell which arm they put in first; but as soon as they undertake to do the thing, the arm which commonly goes first makes its movement; and it is only by a strong act of will that it can be made to give way to the other.

Consider, again, the handwriting. This depends in part upon the structure of the hand, and perhaps also upon one's mental tendencies; but habit has a great deal to do with it; and we all know how difficult it is to disguise one's hand. Then, too, consider how easily we write with the right hand, and how hard it is to write with the left. When the right hand, however, has become disabled, a man, after long effort, can make his left hand write as easily as the right ever did.

Observe, farther, how skill is acquired in any handi-work, so that at last the work goes on better when we are not thinking of it, than when we attend to what we are doing. The fingers of the skilful pianist take care of themselves, and old ladies can read as they knit. So strong does habit, as the result of training, become, that it is said to be impossible for a good swimmer to drown himself, unless he be tied hand and foot. By habit that has become an instinct, the body practises the lesson that it has learned; and the man who has thrown himself into the water swims in spite of himself.

Notice, now, the good results of this tendency of habits to become fixed. In some cases, like those to which I have referred, *the life of the person is, in a sense, doubled.* As was just said, the old ladies knit and read or talk at the same time. So in very many things, the body that has been trained does the work while the mind is left free to busy itself as it will.

Another great advantage that springs from the fixity

of habits is found in the fact that, by means of this, *our lives may make real progress.* What we have gained is secured to us.

Think how hard it would be if we had continually to start again from the beginning. How the soldier shrinks when he first goes into a battle; how gladly he would flee! It is said that green soldiers are sometimes placed alternately with those that have been seasoned in many a fight, that the stability of the veterans may keep the raw recruits in their place. The old soldiers have got so in the habit of marching and standing as they are told, that it has become with them a matter of course.

Consider, too, how a man who is in the habit of handling money lets it pass through his hands with hardly a thought of the possibility of keeping any of it. In such cases habit may sometimes be a better safeguard than principle that has not hardened into habit. Principle untrained may sometimes give way to a temptation which habit would withstand.

This fact applies to everything that we do, and to every relation of our lives. We can make a habit of honesty, of industry, of kindliness, of attention, of courtesy, and of whatever we will. Indeed, Aristotle, one of the wisest men of antiquity, defined virtue as a habit of rightdoing.

Consider what power we have thus over our lives. We shape them to a large extent as we choose, and then, through habit, they tend to harden into the shape that we have given them, as the plaster hardens into the shape which the artist has chosen.

The matter has, very obviously, another side. Bad habits form as readily as good ones. I am not sure that they do not form more readily than good ones, because virtues require more effort than faults. We drift into faults; but to make the best life, we have to take control of it and guide it.

Think, now, how many bad habits are formed,— habits of inattention, of carelessness, fretfulness, of evil speaking, of selfishness, and others that are even worse. I have in another place spoken of the habit of drunkenness, which comes on so quietly that one does not suspect it until it may be too late.

Indeed, a bad habit is the last thing that most of us are afraid of. We think that we are acting always from our own choice, that it is no matter what we do now, because another time, whenever we wish, we can do differently. But all the while a certain habit is forming and hardening, until at last we find ourselves almost helpless. Thus, even our tastes, our amusements, our selection of books, the tendency even of our most secret thoughts, are becoming fixed, and we are becoming permanently the persons we meant to be only for the moment.

If the artist takes such pains with the plaster that he is forming, so that it may harden into a shape of beauty, what care should we take of the habits which are to effect so strongly and permanently our bodies, our minds, and our hearts.

## CHAPTER XLIV

### TEMPTATIONS.

I THINK that there is nothing which we tend to picture in our minds so falsely as temptations. I should be interested to know what ideas of temptation are held by all who read this little book

We are apt to think of temptation as something black and terrible. Perhaps we think of it as something bat-like, hovering about with wings and horns as Apollyon is pictured in the Pilgrim's Progress. Perhaps the preachers and moralists have had something to do with forming the tendency to think of temptation in this way. They rightly paint it as something terrible, and so we come to think of it as being repulsive in its form as it is dangerous to our lives.

In this way we get such notions of temptation that we fail to recognize it when it actually comes. We say, "O you pleasant and harmless-looking thing, there cannot be anything wrong about you." Thus we give ourselves up to it and follow it wherever it will lead

First of all, you need to fix in your minds that *temptation always presents itself as something extremely pleasant*, or at least desirable. This will be clear if you ask yourself what is meant by a temptation. A temptation is, very obviously, something that tempts. It must, therefore, be something that attracts; that is, that appears to be a very pleasant thing to do. If it did not look pleasant to us, it would not be a temptation. Nobody is ever tempted to do anything that seems unpleasant.

In the next place, you need to fix it in your mind that the temptation *always seems reasonable.* What you are tempted to do seems not merely to be something pleasant; it seems something that is, to a greater or less extent, reasonable.

The pleasantness is indeed sometimes stronger than the reasonableness; that is, a man is so attracted by the thing, that he does it even when his reason tells him it is neither right nor wise. This is, however, in rather extreme cases. Ordinarily, temptation is as plausible as it is attractive.

We see the plausibility of temptation from the fact that every mood and every passion tends to justify itself.

When you are angry without a reasonable cause, you do not say to yourself, " This anger is wrong and unreasonable; I am making a fool of myself, besides giving pain to another." This is not the way in which you reason with yourself when you are in a passion. What you do say to yourself is something like this: " There was never anybody in the world that was treated so badly as I am. That fellow is the meanest, most selfish, and most disagreeable person in the world. There is nobody that would not, if so treated, be as angry as I am. In fact, I am not angry at all. I was never cooler in my life. I see things precisely as they are. I don't care because the thing was done to *me*, I only look at the principle of the thing." This you say, when, perhaps, you are bursting with rage, and when in half an hour you will feel heartily ashamed of yourself.

The boy that is tempted to disobey his parents is apt to put the thing very plausibly to himself. He thinks perhaps that his parents would not really care, or he thinks that it is so little a matter that there can be no harm in it, or he thinks that he knows very much more about the thing than they do; that they forbade him to go on the ice because they thought it was not strong enough, whereas he knows that it is as strong as need be. Or, he thinks that there was never a boy kept so close and so bothered by rules as he is; and that the manly thing is to assert his independence.

In all this you see there are many things that he does not think of. He does not think of what he owes to his parents, of their love and care. He does not think that they have much more knowledge and experience than he; and that, though they may now and then make a mistake, yet this is nothing to the blunders that he would make and the trouble he would bring upon himself, if he were left to look out for himself. He does not think of the *duty* of obedience.

A young man in business is tempted to take some money that belongs to his employer. We saw in a former chapter how the imagination leads him on to commit the theft. We now have to see how plausible the temptation may appear.

The young man thus tempted thinks that his employer will not miss the money; that he will be just as well off without it as with it, while to himself it will be everything. Then the amount is so small that it really is no great sin if he takes it. Above all, he thinks that it is only a loan. He needs it only for a little time, and then he will restore it; there can certainly be no great harm in that. He perhaps takes the money, and after a while he is tempted to make a similar "loan." He goes through the same reasoning as before, except that now he is deeper in debt, and he thinks that if he does not take a little more now he will never be able to pay back that which he took before. Finally he takes still more as a matter of self-defence. He will be ruined if he does not. It is no longer a matter for argument. It can hardly be called a temptation It is a necessity. Then, perhaps, when he persuades himself that it is too late to turn back, he admits, for the first time, that he is, what he has been all along, namely, a thief.

Such examples might be multiplied indefinitely, for all temptation is attractive, and nearly all temptation is plausible.

This is one of the most important things to be borne in mind. Knowing under what disguise temptation conceals its ugliness and its sin, we may be on our guard that we are not imposed upon by it, and do not take it for granted that because a thing seems so attractive and reasonable it must therefore be right.

Temptation may be a help as truly as a hindrance. If it comes to us without our seeking, resistance to it may strengthen our moral fibre, just as meeting and conquering any physical or mental obstacle may strengthen our bodily or mental fibre. Emerson says: " As the Sandwich Islander believes that the strength and valor of the enemy he kills passes into himself, so we gain the strength of the temptation we resist." [1]

It must be remembered, however, that when one throws himself willingly in the way of temptation, he shows that he is already half prepared to yield to it

---

[1] " Compensation," in the first series of Essays.

## CHAPTER XLV.

### THE CONSCIENCE.

THE conscience is that within a man which, if he is tempted to do wrong, often warns him and strives to hold him back.   If he persists in the act, conscience often makes him very uncomfortable while it is being done, and when the deed has been accomplished reproaches him for his fault.

Conscience is thus placed to be *the guide of our life.* We may compare it to the private oracle of Socrates, of which I have already spoken.   Or, we may compare it to the compass, which is placed in a ship in order that by it the sailors may control their course.

Nothing in our lives can be more important than that we should attend to the voice of conscience, and obey it; disobedience to it means the ruin of our lives.

Yet there is scarcely anything of which men are more heedless, so far as care for it is concerned, even if they pay more or less attention to its warnings.

Consider how careful the sailors are of the compass by which they are to steer the ship.   The compass, you know, does not point exactly north and south; it varies a little according to the part of the world where it is.   It is more or less affected by what is about it. The iron that is in the ship affects it, and makes its irregularity greater.   If all this were not known and thought of, the compass might lead the ship to its destruction. But it is all thought of. The variation of the needle is taken into the account. An extra compass is sometimes placed at the mast head, far above any disturbance from the iron that enters into the construction of the ship, in order that there it may follow its own laws.

The conscience, like the compass, has its variations. It does not always point straight to the right. Sometimes, in critical moments, it fails to give any indication whatever.

Surely these irregularities are worthy of the most careful study. Let us consider some of them.

*The conscience is sometimes wholly silent when we have most need of its guidance.*

Perhaps the greatest number of our faults are those of omission and carelessness. In moments of pure thoughtlessness the conscience is inactive; and yet it is in these moments that we often need it most.

Suppose that a man has some important duty to perform. He is perhaps the captain of an ocean steamer. His vessel is in critical circumstances, and needs his care. He goes down to his dinner, gets interested in talking with his passengers, and forgets his ship, until it is too late.

It is through such neglect that many bad habits obtain the mastery over men. They come from pure thoughtlessness; and conscience gives no warning.

Acts of cruelty often spring from thoughtlessness. The person speaks or acts without thought, and the conscience has no opportunity to protest.

How much damage is done by pure heedlessness. The boy does not mean to do any harm, but the harm is done. If it were anything wrong that he was *making up his mind to do*, conscience would speak; but at what moment could it interfere in this time of utter carelessness?

It is worth while to remember, then, that during so large portions of our life conscience sleeps at its post. It is at times, too, in which we most need its guidance, for they are full of peril and temptation.

Knowing this failure of conscience, *we should take it into our calculation*, as the sailor takes into his calculation the irregularity of his compass. We should provide against danger by taking measures in advance for our protection.

It is one of the most remarkable things in our natures, that *we can govern ourselves even in these moments of carelessness*. A boy, for instance, starts to go to school. He starts early so as to give himself time to play by the way. Having this time, he stops to play. In all this there is nothing wrong. But in his play he forgets his school, and so arrives tardy, or not at all. How can this tardiness and all similar results of heedlessness be prevented?

The trouble with the boy was that he did not fix it with sufficient force in his mind that he must be at school at the proper hour. If he had done this, issuing to himself a peremptory command, the force of this command would have been felt even in his thoughtlessness and play; and the impulse which he gave to himself at starting would have brought him safe to school at its opening.

Knowing, then, that we are thus exposed, through thoughtlessness, to do what we shall afterwards wish had not been done, or to neglect what we shall wish had been done, we should, in advance, *issue our commands to ourselves;* and if these commands are given earnestly, the self, even in our forgetfulness, will be pretty sure to obey.

Conscience often fails to warn us when we are doing wrong, because we persuade ourselves that what we are doing is not wrong. In the chapter on temptation we have seen that every mood and every passion tends to justify itself. This plausibility of temptation does much to silence the voice of conscience.

In one way the conscience comes to our help in these matters. After the fact, it often reproaches us with our wrong-doing or our neglect. We feel that our carelessness was wrong, perhaps even a crime or a sin. This after-thought is one of the most important of the means by which conscience trains us. We had not dreamed the thing was wrong till we feel the reproach. Being impressed in this way by conscience that we have done wrong, we shall find it easier at another time to remember and to avoid the offence.

Thus one speaks a word that gives pain to another. Seeing the pain that he has caused, he reproaches himself with his carelessness or his ill-temper. This reproach is the voice of conscience. The person has learned a lesson; namely, that such cruelty, whether

designed or not, is wrong   Another time, he may remember this lesson, and keep back the sharp and poisoned speech.

All this suggests another way in which conscience
may come to fail us in our hour of need.   *If we do not
heed its voice, it will tend to become silent* and leave us to
ourselves.   In this respect it may be compared to some
delicate tool   A boy has a good jackknife given to him.
He is pleased with the gift and begins to use it on
everything.   He tries to cut pieces of wood that have
knots in them ; or brings its edge even against nails
The knife, being forced thus against what will not yield,
becomes dull and jagged, and finally refuses to cut anything.   When we do not heed our conscience, we ourselves are the hard bodies by which it is dulled and
made useless.   Or we may compare it to a magnet,
which, if it is not used, tends to lose its power, and to
become like any other bit of steel.

Another way in which the conscience loses its power
is *through the influence of bad companions.*   We have
seen, in another chapter, how much we are influenced
by those with whom we associate.   We tend to
forget that what we become accustomed to see and
hear is wrong.   We come to think that we can do
without harm what others do.   Thus we quiet our conscience, and it ceases for a time, at least, to trouble us

Some may think, perhaps, that it is a great thing if
they can thus get rid of so troublesome a companion.
Two things are, however, to be remembered.

One is, that though the conscience may be put to sleep

for a time, *it may sometime awake.* Though we may avoid its guidance, perhaps we may not always avoid its reproaches. The second is, that one who has lost his conscience *has lost the best part of his manhood.*

I am sure, however, that most will feel that the conscience is a thing to be watched and guarded and obeyed, as the sailors watch and guard and obey the compass which is their guide, that thus the voyage of life may be, in the truest sense, a successful one.

## CHAPTER XLVI.

### CONCLUSION.

THIS little book is simply an introduction to the study of Ethics. At its close it may be well to glance for a moment at some of the elements that enter into this study when it is pursued more fully.

One part of Ethics consists in considering *the relation between morality and religion,* how far morality is helped by religion and generally affected by religion. This is a very important matter for consideration.

There is also to be studied *the philosophy of morality,* what are its fundamental principles, and what is the basis upon which it finally rests, and what is its relation to our thought of the world in general.

There is also *the history of Ethics.* This consists of two parts. One is the history of the various theories about morality, and the other is the history of morality itself, showing the stages through which different peoples have passed in their moral life, and the historical origin and development of the different virtues.

There is also what is called *applied Ethics.* This, also, may have two parts. In one it may consider, as we have been doing, only much more fully, what is the true life for individuals. In the other part, it considers the application of Ethical principles to the world at large, and seeks to discover what are the best methods of charity and reform.

This last is a very important aspect of Ethical study. There is much suffering in the world from poverty and crime; and one of the most pressing needs of the world to-day is that those who have the good of others at heart should find out the best way of lightening or removing these evils. I hope all who read this little book will take an interest in this branch of Ethical study, and will do something to make the world better and happier.

CPSIA information can be obtained
at www.ICGtesting.com
Printed in the USA
LVOW03s2150140816

500384LV00013B/100/P

9 781297 297403